DEVON LIBRARY SERV
Please return this book on or before the la
Book loans may be renewed by p

GW00738145

BOYS

Nick Fisher has been a freelance journalist for ten years, working for a wide variety of teenage and women's magazines and newspapers. He is the resident agony uncle for *Just Seventeen* and also writes scripts for television and radio. He is a mad-keen angler and collects American cars. He is 32, and currently lives in east London with his wife Helen and whippet Ollie.

BOYS
ABOUT
BOYS

The Facts, Fears
and Fantasies

NICK FISHER

PAN

For Nellie

First published 1991 by Piccadilly Press, London

This Pan edition published 1993 by
Pan Macmillan Children's Books
a division of Pan Macmillan Publishers Limited
Cavaye Place London SW10 9PG
and Basingstoke

Associated companies throughout the world

ISBN 0 330 32593 0

Copyright © Nick Fisher 1991

The right of Nick Fisher to be identified as the
author of this work has been asserted by him in accordance
with the Copyright, Designs and Patents Act 1988.

Illustrations by Harry Venning

All rights reserved. No reproduction, copy or transmission
of this publication may be made without written permission.
No paragraph of this publication may be reproduced, copied or
transmitted save with written permission or in accordance with
the provisions of the Copyright Act 1956 (as amended). Any
person who does any unauthorized act in relation to
this publication may be liable to criminal prosecution
and civil claims for damages.

3 5 7 9 8 6 4

A CIP catalogue record for this book is available from
the British Library

Typeset by Cambridge Composing (UK) Ltd, Cambridge
Printed by Cox & Wyman Ltd, Reading

This book is sold subject to the condition that it shall not,
by way of trade or otherwise, be lent, re-sold, hired out,
or otherwise circulated without the publisher's prior consent
in any form of binding or cover other than that in which
it is published and without a similar condition including this
condition being imposed on the subsequent purchaser.

ACKNOWLEDGEMENTS

Special thanks to Charlotte Owen for her encouragement and expertise. Also thanks to all the *Just Seventeen* readers who have kept me supplied with information and problems.

CONTENTS

INTRODUCTION

The trouble with being a teenage boy is that no one listens to you and no one talks to you. It's a bit like living in a vacuum. A vacuum filled with loads of other teenage boys who share the same severe lack of knowledge.

And the knowledge you lack is just the sort of stuff that you're going to need in 'real life'. Sure, you know loads about how to do a straight-knuckle rabbit-punch, perform a wheelie or do unspeakably dangerous things with bangers. You know these things because they're the 'verbal-currency' of your peers. If you hang around with your mates you can learn how to bend a free-kick or strike a match with your teeth, but none of it's much use for actually steering you through the turbulent teenage years. What you *need* to learn is things like how to communicate with girls, and understand your own feelings.

You also don't learn much about sex. At least you don't learn anything that makes any sense.

When I was 12, I was pretty confused about the specific ins and outs of sex. Of course I'd listened hard in biology and got a good grip on all the chickens-do-this and rabbits-do-that stuff. But it didn't really seem to translate very practically into the world in which I existed, and certainly didn't get me any closer to getting off with a real live girl.

What was hugely confusing apart from anything else was the enormous range of slang that existed in relation to sex. In the classroom it was all proper and correct with references to vaginas, penises, copulation and intercourse. But in the playground it was all gibberish about wanks, fucks, blow-jobs, hand-jobs, fannies and noonies. Not a lot of what was talked about behind the Portakabin in those days made any sense. Partly because it was a pile of made-up, back-slapping, self-bragging cobblers. But also because I, for one, simply didn't understand half of the terminology. And believe me there is absolutely no way that in such a situation any one boy can turn to his mate and say, 'Excuse me, Wayne, what do you actually mean by a "blow-job"?' If he did, he'd have been the laughing stock of the whole school, because he'd have been stupid enough to admit what everyone else was too afraid to confess – that *they* don't really know what they're talking about either!

So where *do* you learn the truth about sex, girls, emotions and stuff when you're male, adolescent and desperately anxious about what people will think?

Parental help and guidance *can* be invaluable but for a lot of boys, the prospect of having an honest and open conversation with a parent about sex seems about as attractive as being caught squeezing your spots by the entire female contingent of the sixth form. Much as you may want to know the right information, there is often a barrier of acute embarrassment created by both parent and son which soon brings any discussion to a close. In many ways it may be easier for girls because mothers accept that they have to explain and educate their daughters about periods and pregnancy in order to protect them. But there is not the same motivation to educate boys. Often the responsibility for a boy's sex education is left to his father, who may be handing down knowledge which wasn't explained to him very well (if at all) in the first place. So the problem is perpetuated.

I was lucky. I had access to three vital sources of information: sisters, sisters' friends and sisters' magazines. I started reading the features and problem pages of my sisters' *Jackie* and *Petticoat* magazines and soon learnt that there was an awful lot that the big boys behind the Portakabin didn't know. The sad thing is that those same boys are now grown men, probably fathers themselves, and I bet there's still a whole truck-load of things that they don't know. Partly because no one ever told them, but also because they were too afraid to ask – since they felt that they already *ought* to know.

For the last five years I've written my own problem page in *Just Seventeen* called 'A Boy's View'. In this I've dealt with thousands of letters from both girls and boys. This book is meant to reflect the sort of questions I get asked, especially by boys, through the distance and anonymity of the advice page, and also to provide some of the answers.

I never intended this to be a text book for strict educational reference. I don't want it to be dry and unreadable. It's meant as a guide and a trigger for further discussion. So the information included isn't meant to be definitive. Instead it gives a general outlook and understanding.

What I *did* want was to write a book that made up the balance between girls' education about sex, that comes from mothers, big sisters and a wealth of useful magazines, and boys' education that comes from a lot of lads telling tales and porkie pies.

As well as from the physical aspects of being an adolescent boy, I badly wanted to tackle some of the emotional and mental pressures too. Because if you think there's a lack of advice and sense from your peers about *sex* – just try talking about *feelings*!

I hope that this book will help all readers – male or female, adult or adolescent. I hope it helps to show that there is a lot going on in the minds of teenage boys that deserves to be recognized and understood. And I hope most of all that it will help boys realize that you don't have to go on living in a vacuum; if there's anything you want to know – it's all right to ask. In fact, it's not only all right to ask, it's *important* to ask.

Nick Fisher

CHAPTER ONE
THE BODY

1. Changes in Adolescence

One of the most striking things that happens to a teenage boy as he reaches puberty is that his body starts to change. And, having your body begin to develop around you in all sorts of unexpected ways can be very disquieting. Here's this thing which you've lived in quite comfortably all your life which suddenly decides to expand, alter and sprout hair with very little warning.

Although girls have to cope with even more physical developments, somehow it seems that they get more help with it. They appear to get more guidance and advice from their mothers than most boys ever get from their dads.

And as if it's not bad enough having to undergo various types of body development yourself, the situation is often made worse by the fact that not everyone necessarily experiences the same changes at the same time. So you might find that your progression into puberty is greatly advanced or indeed much slower than that of your peer group.

As a result, because boys can be so competitive, especially physically, the stages of your adolescent development can become a major issue. Boys who are very advanced might become bigheaded and over-confident whereas boys who have developed much more slowly might begin to feel inadequate.

Sadly, some boys believe that at 13, the size of your penis, density of pubic hair and depth of voice in some way denotes how much of a man you are.

Luckily, though, within a few years everyone's voice will have broken, hair will have grown, and so on. However, that doesn't take away the tension and difficulty of those adolescent years.

Spots

If spots are going to be a problem in your life, you can be sure that they will start in your teenage years. Some people claim that you will grow out of them, but that's not entirely true. Invariably they do get better as you grow older, but they don't necessarily go away. Nearly everyone experiences spots at various times through their life; spots are by no means only endured by teenagers.

The trouble with spots if you are a boy is that you don't really have too much of an idea of how to deal with them. Whole sections of girls' magazines are dedicated to giving useful hints on skin care, whereas boys are left to muddle through on their own.

Doctors and chemists are invariably very helpful though, when approached for suggestions and treatment. It may seem like a big deal to you, to go to one of these professionals about your spots, but to them you're just another patient. ther you're a boy or a girl makes little or no difference e treatment is exactly the same. So, advice and t are available if you're prepared to go out and ask

anliness are probably the two most significant

factors which affect spots. If you eat too much processed food or too much sugar you may aggravate your skin. Similarly if you don't wash your skin regularly and thoroughly you will allow harmful bacteria to grow.

Unfortunately a lot of boys might think that it's cissy or unmasculine to use facial cleanser or buy medicated spot creams. But it's a fact of life that if you are prone to spots, keeping your skin clean and bacteria-free will reduce their chances of eruption.

Spots can be a major source of depression and upset, because they make us aware and self-conscious of our facial image. It makes sense then to take a regular course of prevention, rather than just trying to deal with them every time they appear.

Body odour

As boys turn into adults, it is perfectly normal for their bodies to develop in shape and musculature. As they fill out in size and form, they may also grow more body hair. Connected to this development is the change in body odour.

The sweat glands develop along with the changing musculature in order to control the temperature of the body. This results in more sweat being produced, especially if the body is being used more actively or athletically.

The smell of sweat, especially if it is stale, can be very acrid and unpleasant, so it is important to be aware if this change is occurring.

Wearing man-made fibres or non-porous fabrics can hinder the flow of fresh air to the skin. This, coupled with the presence of more perspiration due to the sweat glands working harder, can lead to a much stronger body odour. Therefore natural fibres are preferable.

Similarly, socks can become pretty unpleasant things too, especially if worn inside synthetic trainers day in and day out. So they should be changed at least once a day, as should underwear.

It is also essential to wash and change clothing regularly, and perhaps use anti-perspirant deodorant on especially smelly areas, for instance under the arms.

Hair

To girls it must seem strange that boys can get so concerned and anxious about how much hair they have and where it is. Many girls seem to spend interminable hours with wax and natty devices trying to rid their bodies of excess hair. Whereas boys write to me by the score pleading for me to recommend a magic lotion that'll cause thick bushy fuzz to sprout on their chins, groin, chest, underarms and legs simultaneously.

Pubic and underarm hair are the first visible signs of reaching puberty for boys, so it identifies the start of physical maturity and manhood. In the same way that girls will long for their breasts to start growing, so do boys pray for a suitable bush to form. It's a visible token of manhood – a boy can parade around the changing rooms, as if to say, 'Look at me – I'm a *man!*'

What grows or doesn't grow on the chin is even more important though. Many girls admit to having padded out their first bras in order to give the illusion of having a larger bust than they really did. In exactly the same way, loads of boys pretend they need to shave long before they actually do.

'I must have been shaving for about two years before I ever had to. Twice a week I would stand in the dorm lavatories and make a big show of it. I had all the kit;

*foam, brush, razor and all that but nothing on my chin
but bum fluff.'*

Adam (19)

All around the country there are boys who religiously go
through the ceremony of soaping up, scraping away, rinsing
off and then splashing on after-shave for no practical reason.
More often than not there is nothing resembling stubble
that needs to be removed. There is only a vain hope that if
you do it enough times something might miraculously start
to grow. In reality it's just an example of wanting to look
and feel adult.

Voice breaking

One of the physical changes that occurs when boys reach
the age of puberty is that their voice will change. 'Voice
breaking' is the term used to describe this development
which usually happens around the age of 14.

In fact, nothing actually breaks. What does happen is
that the testosterone hormone, which is the male hormone
secreted into the bloodstream by the testes (the balls),
causes the larynx or voice box to grow larger.

As the larynx grows, the vocal chords which are strung
inside it become thicker and longer which has the effect of
lowering the tone of the voice.

Normally this development will pass largely unnoticed.
Boys may not realize that their voice has changed at all,
because the progress has been so gradual.

Some may feel a roughness or tightness in the throat for
a few weeks and find that their voice becomes a little
croaky. This will soon pass, though, leaving them with a
deeper tone to their voice than they had before.

Balls dropping

Another myth that is regularly bandied about is that when teenage boys reach puberty, suddenly their balls drop down into their scrotum and they become fertile men. This is nonsense.

There is nothing sudden about your balls descending into your scrotum, in fact the process starts before you are born. The descent of the testes from the groin down into the scrotum usually happens naturally, although very rarely one or both of the balls may not descend. This can be rectified by a very simple operation.

As you grow older, the penis and testes go through various stages of development. Around the age of 11 or 12 the scrotum and penis will begin to gradually grow. The skin around the balls will appear to become looser and baggier and the penis may thicken and swell. The changes that take place are slow and gradual so it's not something that you'll necessarily notice, no matter how diligently you keep checking. And you certainly won't wake up one day to discover that your genitals have been transformed overnight.

Within a year or two, at around 13 or 14, pubic hair will also begin to form around the base of the penis, and one testicle (usually the left one) will hang lower than the other. The testicles will probably not grow at the same rate, so one may always appear larger.

As puberty passes, the density of pubic hair will increase and so will the size of the penis and testicles.

Many boys will also notice a gradual change in colour of the skin around the scrotal sac as it thickens and grows. For fair-skinned boys the scrotum will appear reddish in colour and with darker skinned boys the scrotum will be noticeably darker than the rest of their body. This is perfectly normal.

Wet dreams

Wet dreams are often one of the first experiences of sexuality that a boy may have. A wet dream is the name given to the occurrence of ejaculating sperm while sleeping. It simply means that a boy may climax unconsciously and so wake up in the morning to find a patch of wet semen on the bedclothes.

One of the most frustrating things is that very, very rarely can you remember what the dream which aroused you so much was actually about! So often it is such a deeply subconscious event that the only evidence you have of it is the wet patch.

Like all other dreams, wet dreams are elusive, you can't control them, predict them or avoid them. Some males have them regularly right through their teens and on into adulthood. Some males only have a few and then stop. Others never experience them at all.

The most likely period for them to occur is during early adolescence when a boy's sexuality is developing. They act as a subconscious release of sexual tension, yet they are not related to any sexual problem. If boys have lots of wet dreams it doesn't mean they are over-sexed or very frustrated, it merely means that they have healthy and active subconscious minds. But nor does the absence of wet dreams mean a lack of interest in sex.

Wet dreams are absolutely normal and natural, they can be a bit embarrassing and maybe upsetting when they first happen. They can also be a bit annoying if they happen regularly, but invariably their frequency will decrease and they eventually go away completely or occur only occasionally.

It seems strange that for many boys, their first sexual event should happen unconsciously without planning or device. But this does in a way underline how natural, innocent and deep-seated a person's sexuality really is. It exists within us whether we want it to or not. Wet dreams should be seen as a pleasure not a problem.

2. Health

Genital health and cleanliness

Although boys make a lot of fuss about their penis, many of them do not know how to look after it and keep it healthy.

Apart from masturbation and urination, some boys don't really think about the state of their penis and testes (balls). And in the same way that some boys are careless and unthinking about having regular baths or changing their socks, they often ignore their penis.

There is a loose covering of skin that runs the length of the penis and when rolled back it will reveal the shiny helmet of the penis underneath. This loose skin is known as the foreskin. Under this skin, a great deal of bacteria and germs can quickly grow, and a white, lumpy substance called smegma forms.

Smegma is not nice stuff, it is basically made up of dead skin cells, bacteria, sweat and it smells horrid. So obviously it is important for the penis to be washed at least twice a day to keep it clean and free from bacteria.

The reason males have foreskins presumably relates back to an era when man stomped the earth unclothed and so the thick skin covering the sensitive smooth skin of the penis helmet was its only protection. Now, we don't need that sort of protection, so the foreskin has become a fairly redundant part of a man's anatomy.

Circumcision

It is very common for men to have no foreskin at all, because it has been removed when they were very young in an operation known as circumcision. Males may be circumcised for a variety of reasons. Sometimes the skin is too tight and will not roll back easily. Or for religious reasons, for instance all male members of the Jewish faith are circumcised. British males aren't necessarily circumcised but in the USA, nearly all males are as a matter of course. This is really only due to social and medical trends as in most cases there is no physical need to remove the foreskin.

An advantage of circumcision is that the lack of foreskin means there is not the same area for trapping bacteria and so creating smegma. The arguable disadvantage of circumcision is that because the helmet is no longer covered by a protective layer, the shiny soft skin becomes tougher and so less sensitive, through continual rubbing against clothing and underwear. It is totally normal and acceptable to have either a circumcised or non-circumcised penis. And sexually speaking most girls do not state that they have any preference, most say they are totally unaware of there being any difference.

The most important factor is cleanliness.

Menstruation

In general girls seem to have a better understanding and knowledge of their genitals and how to keep that part of their body healthy, because they are forced to be aware of them from an early age.

Usually around the early stages of their teens, girls start to experience menstrual periods. These periods happen once a month and commonly last for about a week. Physically what happens is that during the monthly cycle, the womb is preparing for the fertilized egg. At the end of the cycle, when no egg is implanted in the womb, the lining of the womb sheds and renews itself. When this occurs, a trickle of blood seeps out through the vagina.

When a girl starts having periods, it means that she has reached an age of physical maturity called puberty. One of the effects of having these periods is that she has to learn either to insert small cylindrical cotton wads called tampons which are placed into the vagina to soak up the blood, or to use sanitary towels which are absorbent pads that fit inside the panties and lie against the vaginal opening.

Girls are thus forced to have contact and awareness of their genitals, they are given a very clear sign that their bodies are maturing and they are developing into women. Boys on the other hand do not receive such well defined lessons on their physical and genital/sexual development.

Most girls say they are glad and even proud when they start having periods because it gives them a feeling of growing up and progressing into adulthood. Some girls have even admitted that they lied at school and said they had started before they really had in order to impress their classmates.

Although menstrual periods mark an important development in a girl's maturity, they do have their drawbacks. Many females suffer from pre-menstrual syndrome or pre-menstrual tension (PMT). This refers to a time, usually between one or two days before the period starts, when the hormonal activity in their body has the effect of making them moody and irritable. This mood swing can be very severe in some women and may also be accompanied by stomach cramps, headaches, swollen breasts, over-sensitive nipples and various other uncomfortable sensations. Some women, on the other hand, have only mild discomfort.

And during her period a girl may feel more vulnerable and fragile than she normally does. Wearing a tampon or a sanitary towel can understandably affect her desire to go swimming, do strenuous exercise and of course, have any sexual contact that involves the vaginal area. Males should be sympathetic to women about periods.

Sexually transmitted diseases (including AIDS)

'When I showed the redness and blotches round the base of my helmet to someone at gym, he said I must have caught a dose of clap or something. Now I'm really scared.'

Callum (15)

There are certain forms of disease like herpes, gonorrhoea, syphilis and non-specific urethritis which are only or mainly transmitted through direct sexual contact.

When you have unprotected or unsafe sex, i.e. when you are not wearing a condom, you run the risk of catching a sexually transmitted disease. The HIV virus (Human Immunodeficiency Virus) which may develop into AIDS is one of the viruses which are carried in bodily fluids such as menstrual blood, ordinary blood, semen, breast milk or faeces (shit). Any exchange of these fluids during sexual intercourse may transmit infection. And sexually transmitted diseases all sort of work together anyway. If you're suffering from one form of infection, your ability to resist new infections will be greatly reduced. So, if you've already caught something, you actually run a greater risk of catching something else if you continue to have unsafe sex.

The HIV virus, which is the most potentially dangerous of the sexually transmitted diseases (STDs), may be carried by a man or a woman and there is no visible way of telling if someone has it. A person may be infected with the virus yet show no symptoms whatsoever. The HIV virus is actually very fragile, however, which means that it cannot survive for long in the open air on its own. Therefore it is impossible to catch the HIV virus off cutlery, toilet seats, etc, or by 'dry' kissing or shaking hands. The virus lives in the body, so the only way to exchange it is through bodily fluids. Consequently, by using condoms during sex you can greatly diminish your chances of contracting HIV or any other STD.

There have been very few recorded cases of HIV being transferred from one person to another during heavy 'wet' kissing sessions. For the virus to be passed there has to be an open cut or cold-sore on both parties' mouths in order for blood to be exchanged. Obviously, the chances of this occurring are very slight – but it is possible.

The virus is carried in blood. Oral sex where there may be menstrual blood present, carries a considerable risk. Whereas male oral sex (a blow-job), in which only semen is passed and providing there are no cuts present, is less of a risk, because then the virus carried in the sperm has to be ingested through the digestive system, which is more likely to kill it off.

Very basically, the risks of HIV are multiplied by the number of partners you choose to have sex with. And the choice of those partners is critical too. You may choose to sleep with only one person, but if they've had numerous previous partners or even one previous partner who themselves had numerous ones, then you enter into a network of potential risk.

More than ever before it is essential that you choose who you have sex with very carefully. The potential for danger is so much greater and the risks so much higher that it's imperative you don't treat sex lightly.

More than ever before we actually need to stop being secretive and coy about sex, we need to be honest about it, purely for our own protection.

Sex is already a very complex and difficult area for us to

navigate through, what with it being weighed down by embarrassment and taboo, but now it's even more tricky because it carries a potentially fatal risk.

Going to the doctor

'I'm too shy to go to the doctor about my problem because I'd have to show him my penis and he's an old friend of my mum and dad's so I couldn't do it. I'd die.'

Paul (14)

On my advice page I receive so many letters from boys who want my opinion on various matters to do with lumps, bumps or warts on their penis which they say they are too embarrassed to show to a doctor.

Similarly, they will write complaining about itches and rashes that have developed after some sexual encounter, but will explain that they can't go to a doctor because of the way in which they contracted the ailment. All this is madness. Your doctor is the one person whom you should *always* first approach about any medical matter, and the fact that it is concerning the genitals makes no difference.

To be blunt, your average doctor sees various sets of genitals day-in and day-out; nothing you can show him or her will surprise or embarrass them. They are totally numb to it all – to them it's just part of the job.

Any medical ailment of any kind, especially when it is something as important as a genital problem, should immediately be referred to your doctor. Don't wait around and procrastinate. In medical matters they are the experts. Discussing or showing your problems to mates is all very well, but don't expect particularly sound advice.

Having a good relationship with your doctor is vital. He or she can be so important in keeping you healthy and giving you peace of mind. Doctors are also sworn to confidentiality, so there is no way they will communicate anything you've disclosed to them to anyone else. And they are professionals; professionals trained to deal with everything from penile warts to athlete's foot without batting an eyelid. If for some reason you don't like your doctor, or can't talk to him/her, you should swap doctors.

CHAPTER TWO
SHYNESS

There is a traditional image of the male of the species which not only suggests the things he should be, like strong and courageous and capable, but also the things he shouldn't be. Shyness is one of those things.

It's a sad fact of life, but many boys learn to hide and cover up aspects of their character that they believe to be

uncool. A lot of boys consider shyness to be a weak and
wimpish defect, and therefore necessary to disguise.

1. What is Shyness?

*'When I want to make a good impression on some people
or one person then I start to think I'm going to make a fool
of myself and immediately I get really shy and clam up.'*
                                                    Dermot (15)

Shyness is about self-image. It's a process in which you
project your own thoughts and self-doubts on to other
people. And you assume that others are sizing you up for
what you say or what you do. The sensation of feeling
socially out of your depth can have the effect of turning all
your worries in on yourself.

Am I saying something really daft?
Does my voice sound weird and squeaky?
Do I look all right?
Am I standing funny?
Am I being a prat?

All these sorts of questions and many more can suddenly
rush through your head when you start to feel uncomfortable and self-conscious.

2. What Sort of Situations Make You Feel Shy?

*'When I'm out with a load of people and I haven't talked
for ages then I start to think that I'm not going to be*

*able to open my mouth as I'll not think of anything good
to say.'*

Alan (15)

*'Meeting new people – that's when I'm at my worst.
Especially if they're a bit older or trendier than me.'*

Daniel (14)

*'Loud people make me feel shy as do people who crack
jokes and try to be funny all the time.'*

Lee (14)

These three examples are all from boys who find that social
situations where there are several people to contend with
are the worst. But it isn't always numbers that are frightening, for many boys (and girls) find that age gaps can cause
them to feel unsure of themselves.

*'Teachers and other kids' parents get me shy. I don't
know what to say to them that would be interesting and
if I stay quiet I get more nervous.'*

Lionel (14)

An awful lot of boys will admit (quietly) to having felt
really shy in the presence of a girl whom they found
stunningly attractive. And every boy (if you can get them
to be honest) will confess to being shy of girls in general at
a variety of different times:

*'Some girls make me feel shy, for instance if I'm walking
down a street and I see a lot of girls talking together
and I know one of them. I get shy talking to her because
I know what her friends are thinking.'*

Alastair (13)

> *'You never know what girls are thinking. My girl-friend's friends are always hanging about in a bunch. They'll just start laughing really loud or whispering and giggling like everything's a private joke. I hate it. You don't even know if they fancy you or think you're duff.'*
>
> Michael (14)

In the same way that a party full of strangers can be frightening and off-putting, so can a group of people, even if you know all or some of them. It can be made even worse because you are the only male among a tight-knit group of females.

Although it is far easier to relate to a member of the opposite sex on a one-to-one basis as opposed to in a group, it's still no piece of cake.

A lot of boys write to me expressing the fear and numbing shyness that overcomes them when they find themselves face to face with a girl.

> *'I feel my face and my head getting hotter, like I must be blushing very badly. And I can't find the right words or think of things to say so then I will just go quiet.'*
>
> Sean (15)

> *'I don't know what boys say to girls when they go out on dates. I'd like to know what they talk about. I'm all right having a laugh and a skit with girls but I don't know how to talk for a long time, like.'*
>
> Colin (15)

With most people, shyness is not necessarily a constant thing. Some days are worse than others, and some situations can seem a doddle one day and yet the next they are fraught with embarrassment and worry. We all have our own individual shy-areas, the trick is knowing the situations which you find difficult and learning to deal with them.

3. How To Cope With Shyness

Shyness itself can be very attractive. What *can* be immensely unattractive are the things that some boys do to cover up their shyness and to compensate for it, like being very loud, very cheeky, sarcastic and showing off.

> *'I try and present myself as a likeable, pleasant person who wants to get on with whoever I'm with. I put myself forward, otherwise you are thought of as stupid and hard to get on with.'*
>
> *Graham (16)*

> *'I just jump straight in and if they think I'm an idiot it's up to them.'*
>
> *Charlie (13)*

> *'I'll be as talkative and trendy as possible. I try to put shyness aside and forget about it.'*
>
> *Joe (14)*

These boys have all learnt to cope with their shyness by forcing themselves to deal with the social situation they're up against and going for it, regardless. In this way they are able to block out any feelings of shyness and insecurity by talking fast and putting up a front.

The risk you run in taking this approach is that you go over the top and talk too fast, put up too big a front, too loudly, which will not only have the effect of scaring people away, but will do you no real justice, because the image you put forward is not what you are really like deep down.

There is no right or wrong way to deal with shyness, everybody has to develop a technique that suits them and suits the particular situation they are in. But it is important to realize that basically *everyone* is shy. Everyone suffers from insecurities, self-doubts and lack of confidence. Some people cope with it better and some people can put on a good act of pretending that they are not shy.

However there are ways of helping yourself:

Body language

There are certain types of body language that are a give-away of being shy: for example, folding your arms across yourself or hugging yourself, fiddling, avoiding eye-contact or standing with one foot entwined around the other leg all give the impression of insularity. They look as though you're trying to trap yourself in and so close yourself off to the outside world.

If you study apparently confident people, their body language is much more open, they may swing their arms about and gesticulate and keep eye contact as they talk. Even if you don't feel confident, you can always *act* confident by imitating the physical moves and patterns of a confident person. This is role-playing – you are acting in a way you'd naturally like to be.

Also, if you make yourself laugh easily, smile readily and keep steady eye contact with the people to whom you are talking, this automatically gives you an air of confidence.

One of the most important things which this sort of confident role-playing does is it takes you out of yourself. It is important to be aware of the fact that you are experiencing shyness and to take note of these feelings. But it is counter-productive to dwell too much on self-scrutiny, when you are actually in a social situation. This can have the effect of making you more shy and self-conscious.

Focusing on others rather than yourself

Instead what you should do is focus your attention on other people. Ask questions, solicit other people's opinions on things and give them the opportunity to talk. If you listen and concentrate on what they are saying rather than on what you are feeling, you may forget to be shy altogether.

The trick is to give yourself the impression of confidence.

Preparing in advance

There are some situations where there's something you want to say, some message you want to convey, and you just *know* it's going to be difficult. It might be when you're going to ask a girl out or even when you want to end a relationship. It could be when you want to ask a big favour or else impart some really serious news. Whatever the situation, if it's scary and worrying, rehearse it.

Although it sounds mad, there is absolutely no better way for preparing to tell someone something than actually going over it in your mind and then saying it aloud, to the mirror, to the dog, to *anyone*.

It's far easier to dry up or say something ridiculous if you haven't prepared yourself than it is if you've gone through it in your mind a couple of times and even given it a once-over out loud.

In a slightly different way, I personally think it's a really good policy to prepare and inspect your feelings sometimes, especially if there's something you think you want to explain to someone, but haven't really decided how you feel about it.

It's often a good idea to write things down as the actual process of writing involves thinking at a slower, more methodical pace. This can have the effect of ordering things more distinctly in your mind and can make answers appear more accessible.

Often people mention at the end of letters sent to my column in *Just Seventeen* that they feel better just for having got what's been rattling round in their heads on to paper.

Another very useful application for writing is when you want to say something to someone but can't find the courage to say it to their face. Sending a letter which clearly explains the way you feel can be an excellent way of communicating something important. First, because you can take your time composing the letter and so make sure that you include everything that you want to cover. Second, because the physical distance of the process means that you can cover subjects which you feel you couldn't broach face to face.

4. Shyness is Not an Excuse

A lot of boys and girls write to me complaining that they are unable to do something because they are too shy. Boys write and say that they're too shy to ask a certain girl out. Girls write and say that they are too shy to ask their boyfriends to kiss them. And both boys and girls write explaining how they can't go to a party, someone's house, a job interview, a night-club, the school disco – or whatever, because they are too shy and worried about what other people will think.

As a result they miss out on certain opportunities which they feel would otherwise be on offer to them. Shyness is a self-centred and debilitating state.

Although we can all relate to feeling shy and we can all sympathize with other people who are faced with social situations that make them feel nervous, it isn't actually an excuse for not doing something.

Giving in to shyness is self-defeating, because it is only yourself that you're fighting against. What other people think and feel is beyond all control. But what isn't beyond all control is our own behaviour, you always have a choice of either joining in and making the best of things, or else doing an impersonation of a wallflower and cowering in a corner.

If you choose to opt out and perpetually sit on the sidelines, then the chances are you'll never really suss out how to deal with the types of situations that make you shy. But if you're prepared to have a go at fitting in and are prepared to take a risk, then you may well make a mistake or two along the way, but eventually you'll learn how to cope with your shyness, and your confidence in these situations will increase.

5. Positive Shyness

'I like shy girls or girls who are a bit shy. I don't feel I have to put on a show and be Jack the Lad all the time.'

Leroy (14)

'I would much rather spend a night out with a lad who was a bit shy than one of those that thinks he's God's gift to women and never stops talking – about himself.'

Nula (19)

Personally, I don't believe that shyness and timidity are an unattractive side to a boy's character. Quite the opposite; it can actually make someone much more endearing, approachable and unthreatening.

CHAPTER THREE
THE MACHO MAN

1. Heroes

'I've got a mate who can take a lock knife or any other sharp knife, lay his hand on the desk, with his fingers all splayed, and stab the knife into the wood really fast between his fingers. He can make it jump from one space to the other like lightning, and he never cuts himself.'

Sam (15)

For some reason boys tend to be attracted to the image of hard men and tough men as heroes because they represent what boys understand as manly characteristics: i.e. strength, courage, power and physical prowess. They are impressed by dangerous stunts, feats of enormous strength and knowledge of violent skills like boxing or martial arts as they all fall into the enviable 'hard man' category.

Unfortunately, all too often when they look for heroes, boys never really look beneath the surface, they focus on what a man *does*; how well he fights, how good he is at football, or how powerful he is.

Rambo, Indiana Jones, James Bond, Bruce Lee and Superman could all be complete bastards, but that wouldn't necessarily prevent boys from admiring them. The prime concern is not what sort of people they are, it's specifically what selection of awesome things they can do.

But it actually makes more sense to judge our heroes and role-models on a deeper level by scratching beneath the surface. Personality, principles and integrity are ultimately worth a lot more than merely having an impressive outer image. We should really pick our heroes because their characters are admirable rather than because their physical abilities are merely awesome.

2. Macho Activities and Behaviour: Myths and Realities

The newsagents can provide an amazing insight into what it is that males are supposed to be interested in. The range of magazine subjects directed at male readership includes: naked women, trains, cameras, cars, hi-fi, fishing, heavy metal, war, weapons and body-building. In essence these are the meat of the macho mind.

All these magazines concern interests which are outside the body, and outside the person. In contrast, women's magazines tend to deal with things that relate and refer directly to the person reading them. You are informed of *your* horoscope, how to use *your* make-up, what clothes would suit *you*, how to evaluate *your* emotions and of course advice pages to write to with *your* problems.

The nearest any male magazine gets to dealing with the person is in a body-building magazine, which of course only ever focuses on the exterior physique and muscles. There is rarely any suggestion that one could work on what goes on inside, on building up your personality and putting a little time into your emotional well-being.

In a lot of ways it is difficult for males because due to the macho image they're not given any scope or encouragement to change and improve in any emotional sense.

On the contrary there's still a lot of pressure from your peer group to act in a 'manly' fashion. This normally includes acting hard and cool; showing no emotion other than the acceptable 'manly' ones like anger or lust.

And the flip-side to this is the sad fact that any boy who *does* show emotion or acts in any way that is different or stylish or against the stereotype gets accused of being 'a poof'.

It seems that in order to defend the 'manly' way that boys behave, they attack anything outside of the norm. And the way they often choose to attack is by making accusations of homosexuality.

This is a sorry state of affairs because it turns homosexuality (which is, after all, just a sexual preference) into something that gets regarded among boys as being negative and wrong. It also scares boys from being honest about their real emotions, fears or feelings in case someone uses this against them in order to have a dig or take the mickey.

Fighting and competition

It seems that boys have to compete right from the start. Most boyhood games are about fighting and conquering. Even if it's Cowboys and Indians or football, the main purpose is always to defeat opponents.

At school, boys are urged to take part in competitive sports in which they are continually trying to out-do each other. Girls play competitive sports too, but a lot of the other games they choose tend to involve a much more defined sense of creativity and togetherness.

Perhaps fighting is the most blatant example of boys' competitiveness. It's very basic and primitive, very animal-like behaviour, similar to stags butting antlers to see who is going to be leader of the pack.

> 'When I first went to my new school I told them all about the boxing I'd done at my old school. I told them how I'd won loads of cups and fought in the ABA Championships, and how I'd been in the local paper because of it. I've never been near a boxing ring in my life, but I knew how to stand right so I'd show off and make up stories. It worked a dream.'

> *Del (16)*

A competitive spirit is not necessarily a bad thing, however it is stupid to boast about achievements, especially if they are untrue.

In the early teens especially, it seems as though the rapid exchange of boasts forms an important part of communication. Boys tend to lie to each other about everything, probably to compete with their peers.

There may not be any real malice in the boasts and untruths which circulate but it is a sign of insecurity which makes them feel that somehow the truth is not enough and so things need to be embroidered and expanded to sound impressive. It is a pity if boys feel they have to exaggerate or lie as it means that their true self and identity are hidden.

> *'My mate's dad's got a brilliant collection of guns. He's got all sorts and some of them are dead old. When he's there he'll let us hold one or two. They're really neat, but me, I want to collect knives. I've got a machete and a bayonet already.'*
>
> *Nick (13)*

Related to this desire of boys to have a he-man image is the fact that a lot of boys have a real lust for weapons of all different types, in order to portray this image. It may also partly be a hangover from the fact that during childhood a great many of the toys which boys receive are imitation weapons, from swords to bows and arrows to plastic sub-machine guns. The result is that a lot of boys grow up with a strong fascination for weaponry which doesn't always seem healthy.

Drinking

> *'We have this game, it's a word game but it's got a forfeit to it. When you get your turn wrong you have to drink a glass of drink. It's just whatever we've got hold of, whisky, vodka maybe, and the winner's the one who can still stand at the end.'*
>
> *Martin (17)*

Alcohol is often central to the macho image and this is perpetuated by massive industries like the advertising business which thrive on telling us that dare-devil

stuntsters drink Carling Black Label and real men are
Tetley drinkers.

There's all that rot about a *real* man being able to hold
his drink and the larger the quantity, the more manly you
must be.

None of it is true. Too much alcohol makes you sick and
piss your pants. That's the reality.

Boys behave badly with booze and many get stupidly
drunk very often. They regard it as another laddish exper-
iment, and think they can prove their manliness by doing
it. The net result is always the same: sick and miserable.
The next day the misery is forgotten in the tall tales about
what a riotous time was had.

But somewhere inside the boy who's bragging and boast-
ing about what a bad lad he was last night, there's a little
voice of sadness and disillusion trying to be heard.

Another disturbing effect which alcohol has on men is
that it can cause a syndrome called 'brewer's droop'. This is
where the intoxicating effect of the booze restricts the male
drinker from being able to gain an erection or have sex. The
sex organs are sensitive and fragile parts of the anatomy,
and not surprisingly they don't function well when the
whole system gets severely doused in alcohol. So if you get
drunk, the chances are you won't be able to have sex that
night.

It's funny, they don't tell you that in the commercials.

*'I got so pissed on cider once that I fell off my bike on
my way home. I fell off on the road and just lay there.
My mate was laughing so much, but then he walked off.
I went on lying there, I wasn't hurt, but I must have
passed out or fallen asleep because suddenly I woke up
and there was this old bloke standing over me. It was
mad. I mean I could easily have been run over by a car.'*
                                                    Nigel (15)

More than anything else, the macho image promotes self-destruction. On the one hand it appears to be all about ego-pumping: if you can fight better, run faster and drink more than your peer group, then you must be a real man and an enviable specimen. You may also have a very sick, diseased liver from too much booze, and no friends. To compete and win is dangerous. To compete and lose is soul-destroying, surely it's far better to forget all the macho-man bollocks and choose not to compete at all?

That way you've got a lot more time to concentrate on learning how to be yourself. And maybe even learning to like yourself, just for what you are, not what you can do.

Drugs

'When I am bored I just think the best thing is to have a few joints and really get off my face. It doesn't harm anyone and it keeps me keen.'

Chris (15)

'Drugs like dope and E are all right because they're party drugs, they're rave drugs. They're not like heroin which is really selfish and vicious. You've got to be sick in the head to do smack.'

Mitchell (16)

Like alcohol, certain drugs seem to have developed a bit of a macho image. Cannabis has become increasingly widely used among teenagers along with newer drugs like Ecstasy.

Both these drugs have become popular as stimulants used 'socially' at raves, all-nighters and parties. As with alcohol there is a rather pathetic notion attached to them that the more you can take and the more mad you behave, then the more of a man you must be.

Cannabis is usually smoked in joints which are passed

around and it causes light-headedness, giggling and sometimes very mild hallucinations. Its short-term side-effects
include memory loss and confusion whereas its long-term
side-effects are not fully known although it can cause severe
paranoia and mental disturbance. Ecstasy on the other hand
is a stronger hallucinogenic and stimulant. Being fairly new
its effects have not been fully investigated, although it has
already been responsible for several deaths through de-
lusion (people jumping off high buildings, etc, in the belief
that they can fly).

Ecstasy is a drug that has developed its own culture. It's
now associated with raves and house music and all-night
partying, so already its image is full of attractive elements.
But the basic truth is that so little is known about the
chemical make-up of the substance or substances that
people are taking when they're dropping 'E's that anything
could be happening. The long-term or even short-term side-
effects are unknown because there hasn't been time to
conduct any useful research.

One image that E seems to have manufactured around it
is the notion that it's a drug that makes you feel sexy and
turned on. In other words it is often thought of as an
aphrodisiac. But, in fact, recent evidence suggests that
although it may heighten some of the sensual perceptions,
it actually inhibits orgasm and may also inhibit erection.
So, from a male point of view, its use as a sexual stimulant
or sex-enhancer is very questionable.

And, of course, on the subject of AIDS and sexually
transmitted diseases, the use of Ecstasy or indeed any drug
before sex is likely to affect badly your sense of judgement
and care. You're far more likely to have unsafe sex if you're
under the influence of intoxicants than if you're straight
and sober.

The other important thing to take on board before decid-
ing to get involved in any way with these drugs is that

Ecstasy and cannabis are both illegal and therefore carry possible prison sentences for anyone found in possession or supplying.

In the same way as alcohol, drugs severely affect your judgement and perception. Under the influence of drugs or drink it is easy to do things which seem very clever or funny but in the cold light of day appear mind-numbingly stupid and embarrassing.

They also give the user a false impression of himself or herself which is divorced from reality. This confusion can lead to serious psychological disorders and dependencies which make users reliant on the drug to make them feel good about themselves.

Using drugs or alcohol does not make you look big or clever, nor does it make you look manly. It can, however, make you look pathetic, out of control and mentally unbalanced.

Swearing

Constantly using swear-words to punctuate sentences is a temptation when you are a teenager. Part of the attraction is its rebellious image. You are not allowed to swear in school, at home or in front of adults. When you are just hanging out with your mates, you don't have to conform to adults' rules; it's like your own personal rebellion against the way that you're forced to behave the rest of the time. And of course, the almost sheep-like nature of lads together means that *everyone* swears like mad, always trying to out-do each other in levels of vulgarity. The fact that most swear-words have sexual connotations makes the whole business feel that much naughtier. Sadly, some boys never grow out of the habit and just go on to be foul-mouthed men instead.

Swearing may have its place and can be effective when used sparingly, at a time that really warrants it. But when used constantly, it is just ugly, clumsy and completely ineffective in terms of conveying any real expression.

When you swear loudly in public, it's just like putting a big label on your head that says 'Yob!' Many people are offended and upset by hearing swear-words. So by using them loudly in public places, not only are you announcing that you don't give a damn about other people's feelings, but you are also giving the impression that you are so immature that you still think that swearing conveys a 'manly' image.

Swearing is another example of boys over-compensating by acting very hard and loud to show their peers what a 'man' they really are. More often than not this is linked to a deep-rooted sense of insecurity that has the effect of causing lads to continually reinforce their manliness and status. It's as though they can't bear just to be themselves without pushing the macho image.

Again this can be linked to a fear of being considered 'soft' or 'gay'. Boys' fears of being accused of homosexual or 'unmanly' behaviour can become so strong (almost paranoid) that they go over the top in order to prove otherwise. It's as though they're too frightened to accept that they, like the rest of us, are made up of a *mixture* of feminine and masculine attributes. And that it is this combination that's so important. Sadly they mistakenly think it's better to prove that they're 'all man'.

3. Big Boys Aren't Emotional

'It is almost scorned by society for boys to express their feelings. Even when we don't realize it. If a boy child falls over, his mother says, "Big boys don't cry!" We're

trained not to be emotional or at least not to show emotions, aren't we?'

Jason (16)

Indeed, some mothers do try to stop their sons from crying from an early age by telling them that they are not supposed to cry; that crying is something which girls do – boys don't. Thus boys learn a very powerful and lasting myth; that it just isn't done for them to show certain emotions. Even if you feel like crying, because you're hurt or you're sad or whatever, you'd be letting yourself and indeed the entire male gender down if you allow that emotion to actually show on the surface. There is a big danger in learning to suppress emotions and hiding feelings, because that means these feelings are never dealt with. Instead, they are simply hidden and held under pressure until they are released in some other totally inappropriate way, perhaps through violence.

How many times do we hear that boxing, football, rugby, etc, are good for boys because it helps them to 'let off steam'? Perhaps there wouldn't be so much pent-up steam and repressed anger if boys allowed themselves to process their feelings as they come up, instead of being told to sit on them and hide them away.

'I feel so frustrated when I want to talk but can't because it's not done, is it? It makes me so angry when someone says, "Oh, keep it to yourself, you'll get over it."'

Simon (15)

The sad truth of the matter is that boys rarely do communicate with one another. They fight with each other, compete, hang out, have a laugh, take the mick, try and out-do each other but it's really a rare occurrence that one teenage boy can sit down with a friend and say: 'This is how I feel . . .'

The problem is self-perpetuating, because even if a boy does manage to overcome his inhibitions and does fly in the face of his keep-it-to-yourself conditioning, there's absolutely no guarantee that the mate he chooses to confide in will be able to cope. When you're brought up to believe that big boys don't cry or get emotional, it can be very disturbing when one of your mates suddenly does!

> *'I think that it is all right for a boy to cry if something really major has happened to him. But you should go home to the privacy of your own bedroom, on your own, and do it there. It's not right to do it in front of your mates.'*
>
> *Steve (14)*

4. Penis Size

There is no other part of the male body that is so steeped in mystery, myth and marvel as the penis. The average penis of a full grown male measures just six inches from pubic bone to tip when it is erect, and when flaccid (not erect) will vary in size enormously depending on things like temperature, humidity and fullness of the bladder.

The number of large penises measuring seven or eight inches long while erect is as rare as the number of small penises, around four inches. So contrary to popular belief, the penis does not really vary much in size from one man to another.

> *'At the swimming pool I've seen other men's penises and testicles and I'm sure that my penis is much smaller*

than average. I haven't had the confidence to go with a
girl because I think I'm too small and I won't be able to
satisfy her.'

Lucien (16)

One popular macho myth is that the bigger the size of
your penis, then the more virile and satisfying you'll be as
a lover. The fact that the penises don't differ much in size
and that many women claim size is not a factor which
relates to a man's ability as a lover, rather stamps on that
theory.

Indeed, penis size seems to be much more of an issue
amongst men than it is with women.

'A good lover has got to be a good kisser. He's got to
have a warm sensual touch, have slow movements, like
hugging and stroking, have a small bottom and a sense
of humour. A big prick is useless if he doesn't have
understanding.'

Marie-Louise (21)

There is no way to increase or diminish the size of your
penis, there are no lotions that'll make it harder and no
potions that'll make it stronger. You get what you're born
with, and if it is erect when you want it to be then the
chances are that you're on to a winner and should just be
satisfied with what you've got. It should be noted that a
penis looks smaller when looking straight down on it, which
might explain why Lucien earlier on thought his was
smaller than average.

5. The New Man

There has been a lot of talk and speculation in recent years about the emergence of the New Man, a breed of male who is sensitive, in tune with women's feelings and generally less selfish and sexist in his outlook.

In certain ways the traditional macho stereotyped image has broken down. For instance, fatherhood roles have changed inasmuch as it is now perfectly acceptable and desirable for a man to be seen pushing a baby carriage, changing nappies and taking care of a child. Similarly, a lot more men now know how to cook, they dress in fashionable clothes, take time and care over their appearance, are much more relaxed and natural in women's company and are beginning to be less afraid to show and admit to their emotions. But there is still a long way to go before men are able to show the more sensitive side to their characters.

Boys should observe and appreciate how women have developed and improved their lifestyles, raised their goals, achieved new ambitions and maintained a unity of purpose between them. Women have done a lot to bring about some level of equality for themselves and now it is about time that men reacted by improving and progressing their own standards.

Machismo is beginning to be seen as outdated; few people – especially women – respect macho-stereotypes.

In terms of commerce and business, it may still be male-dominated, but only just, and not for that much longer. Women have proved in a very short time that they are more than capable of competing and winning in the workplace.

Teenage boys are more than capable of breaking the macho traditions if only they can recognize what an improvement it could make to their personal life, love life, sex life, social life and even work life. Macho behaviour which dictates that you have to act like 'one of the lads' does nothing but alienate the opposite sex. And to a great extent it stops men from progressing and developing because they become locked in a narrow male society that, on its own, is going nowhere.

CHAPTER FOUR
RELATIONSHIPS
WITH GIRLS

1. The Differences Between Boys and Girls

There sometimes seems to be an enormous gap between the sexes which really begins to appear and develop around the age of 8 or 9.

For instance, if you were to observe a primary school class of 5- or 6- or 8-year-olds, more often than not they would seem to be quite equally and thoroughly mixed. The boys and girls will all sit together and freely associate with one another. Yet if you were to return three years later the boys and girls will have segregated.

The segregation seems to develop as a result of differing interests, attitudes and pursuits. In schools, the activities and pastimes which boys and girls follow are different and often social groups develop out of them. A simple example of this is that often the boys go off to play football during breaktime while the girls prefer to sit in the common room and talk. As a result the two sexes are separated.

This is further complicated by the fact that individuals of this age are trying to find and develop their own personal identity. In doing this they are invariably looking for role-models or behaviour they admire in other members of their own sex, which they can then emulate.

The pattern which can develop is of boys hanging around together and following what older boys are doing. The same pattern exists for girls. The separation is essentially a natural thing because boys and girls around the age of 10 or 11 find it easier to identify with their own sex, so they are drawn towards each other. Also girls do mature emotionally earlier than boys and so 11-year-old girls are likely to think that their male counterparts are very young.

The difficulties arise in the teenage years when you want

to reverse the segregation process and start mixing with individuals from the opposite sex.

2. Just Friends or Girlfriends?

Realistically, girl friends come in two categories, girls who are friends, and 'girlfriends'. Girls who are friends are like mates, they're friends you spend time with, who just happen to be girls. 'Girlfriends', on the other hand, imply that you are physically and emotionally involved with them.

This distinction is not carved in stone. Both forms of relationship can be interchangeable; sometimes a boy and a girl who have been mates might find through their contact with each other that something else lurks beneath their friendship and it develops into a romance. Or indeed a relationship may fizzle from being a romantic involvement to becoming a more straightforward friendship. Both forms of relationship are a vital and fulfilling addition to any male's life.

One big mistake a lot of boys make is to assume that there's a world of difference between a friendship with a mate and a relationship with a girl. There isn't. Both rely on common interests, spending time together, being able to talk to each other, laugh with each other and trust each other.

3. Do You Really Want a Girlfriend?

It is generally accepted that girls begin to mature earlier than boys. This means that they reach puberty and adolescence at a younger age and it usually means that they start wanting to have boyfriends before boys of their own age start wanting to have girlfriends. Undoubtedly this is one of the reasons why it is very common for teenage girls to have boyfriends who are a bit older than themselves.

Although boys usually start puberty later than girls, most would like to have a girlfriend eventually. At the same time, they are very, very susceptible to pressure and influence from their friends. This peer pressure can take effect in different ways, for example if all their mates are still wrapped up in football and video games, they might not want a girlfriend, as they might stand out from the herd, while if all their friends are dating girls then they might feel they've *got* to get themselves a girlfriend quickly.

Peer pressure is *not* a good reason for starting a relationship with a member of the opposite sex. A boy who is going out with a girl just to impress his mates is not likely to make a very good boyfriend, because he's obviously going to be more concerned with what they think as opposed to what she feels.

It's nice to find the idea of female company attractive after years of boyishly denying their existence and trying to avoid them at all costs. But it is easy for boys to look on having a girlfriend purely as a status symbol or image-booster.

Relationships that just bring grief are all too common and are ultimately pretty pointless. Where's the sense in having a relationship purely for the sake of it? In fact, it is far more pleasurable and beneficial to remain single and to spend time getting to know and developing your own personality and interests rather than rushing into a relationship.

Teenage magazines and teenage fiction on television are often to blame for urging their readers into believing that love affairs and relationships with the opposite sex are the be-all and end-all of teenage life. They aren't. You don't have to date *anyone* when you are a teenager, and you will still grow up to be a perfectly normal, happy and healthy adult. And in fact the more time you spend on your own, discovering who you are, what are your likes, dislikes, aims and goals in life, when you are a teenager, the more likely you are to sail comfortably on to adulthood.

Friendships with other boys may develop into sexual relationships which may in themselves be purely experimental and only a phase. This sort of sexual experimentation during your teens is by no means a certain sign of homosexuality. An awful lot of boys write to me concerned that they are gay because they've had some sexual experience with a member of the same sex. This is simply not the case.

What may occur is that you want a deeper sort of relationship that is more intimate than the normal laddish acquaintances that you're used to. This may get translated into a sexual act, because that is one form of intimacy. But in time the desired level of intimacy and closeness may then develop with a girlfriend.

It's a desire for this deeper quality of relationship that makes a good reason to get involved in a romance. Wanting to impress your mates that you can 'pull birds' is not a good reason. Nor will it lead to happiness for anyone involved.

4. Talking to Girls

Before you can have a romantic relationship with a girl, some sort of friendship is important. To start a friendship it is necessary to strike up conversation. But this is something that a lot of boys find great difficulty in doing for all sorts of reasons, perhaps because it is a new experience, they are shy, because they think that the things girls are interested in are boring, or that girls will find *them* boring ...

Perhaps the best place to start is to discuss how *not* to talk to girls.

How not to talk to girls

Chat-up lines   Boys often write to me on my advice page and ask me what chat-up lines work. If they existed I would print them everywhere, become a millionaire, and retire to a life of luxurious leisure.

There are no such things as successful chat-up lines, and boys who believe that they do exist are in for a big shock and a long, lonely time.

My friend fancies you   Every week I receive letters from both boys and girls who've caused themselves untold grief and confusion because they've relied on feelings being conveyed by a third party.

> *'I think he fancies me because two of his mates have told me he does. But he never says anything to me, he just ignores me except when there is not many of the others about; then he is a bit friendlier but quite shy.'*
>
> Jenny (13)

There really is no substitute for making your own feelings felt. Apart from the fact that you'll never know how your intentions will be expressed, or who else will get to know along the way, it's also quite insulting. If you care enough about someone and want to get to know them, you should be prepared to put yourself on the line and not hide behind message-carriers. If a girl receives a message or a note, purported to be from you, saying that you really fancy her and want to go out with her, how's she supposed to know it's not just a massive wind-up?

Witty one-liners   A sense of humour is an endearing facet in anybody's personality, but any male who continually comes out with witty one-liners in the belief that they are the way to a lady's heart is definitely barking up the wrong tree.

Cool and aloof   The other side of the coin to the joke-a-minute, whacky-one-liner chat-up champion is the sort of bloke who thinks that the best way to attract a girl is to be cool, aloof and mysterious. This is also rubbish.

Self-obsessed
> *'I get really sick of guys who'll take you out and spend the night talking about themselves. I've been out with ones who talked about their job, their car, their karate lessons and all their ex-girlfriends, but never once asked anything about what I do. It makes me mad. I think it's a real turn-off and extremely rude.'*
>
> Victoria (18)

Communication skills

The way that boys learn to communicate with each other isn't necessarily much help when it comes to communicating with girls. In fact, it can actually be a handicap.

A lot of the time boys don't have what you might call conversations. It's sort of Report-Speech. 'I'll report something funny/scary/unusual that I've seen, heard or thought of and then you tell *me* something.'

The aim is to *impress* each other or whoever else is listening. The responses to 'impressive' statements may well include 'Wow', 'Really?' or 'You're a lying toad'. But they don't necessarily go much deeper, and they don't by any means always develop into a proper conversation.

Striking up a friendship with a girl involves using communication skills which a lot of boys have never learnt, mainly because they've never had to. Their previous friendships have been with members of their own sex where actual *conversation* has never really taken place.

Because a lot of boys rarely talk to each other about anything that is deeply personal they are not well trained in the art of conversation. They are not used to describing their emotions or feelings to one another nor are they practised at just opening up and being vulnerable.

Often they don't have much of a handle on small-talk or chit-chat either, because it doesn't exist within their world of Report-Speech and impressive tales.

In fact they're often much happier doing something that is a focus in itself, rather than having to find a topic for discussion.

> '*At lunchtime all the boys go outside and play football while all the girls stay indoors and just talk all the time. Sometimes if we get the ball stuck on the roof we have to stop, then we might sit and talk. All we talk about though is how to get the ball down off the roof.*'
>
> Steven (13)

On the contrary, girls' friendships seem to function in a different way. They spend a lot less time *doing* things and more time talking about things.

What is actually more important is to make contact, to create some communication which stems from sharing a conversation, not giving a gut-bustin', one-sided, stand-up performance. Indeed when starting a friendship with any girl, the greatest asset a boy can have is not a quick, witty tongue, but an attentive ear.

> *'The best sort of bloke to go out with is the sort who's got a brain and isn't afraid to use it. The sort who can talk about all sorts of subjects, not just football. And who is prepared to shut up and listen from time to time.'*
>
> Yvonne (19)

Conversation is the key, it's the starting point of any relationship with the opposite sex. That doesn't mean it can only be practised on members of the opposite sex, far from it; the 'art of conversation', the ability to speak interestingly, listen attentively and identify similar thoughts, feelings and experiences can and should be perfected by talking with anyone and everyone.

5. Where to Meet Girls

Relationships, especially those between teenagers, normally grow out of existing friendships or acquaintances. Although there's something very romantic in the idea of meeting someone who comes from the other side of the world and then falling desperately in love, it's far more likely that you'll end up going with someone from school or a girl you meet every Wednesday night in the youth club. Contrary to popular belief, discos and nightclubs are not particularly good places to meet people who you'll end up dating. In fact, even in a big city like London, the majority of people have met their partner either through school, college, work or another friend. A great number of people seem to be going out with someone who used to go out with a friend of theirs.

In other words, you don't actually have to scour the four corners of the world to find a soulmate.

6. The First Date

Where to go

'I don't know what to talk about when I'm with her. I think she expects me to be funny or to know places to go and I don't.'

Danny (14)

There are good places to go on dates and there are bad places to go on dates. The best dates are the ones which give you both something to focus on and during which you can be physically quite close.

The cinema is always a good bet for a first date with a girl you don't know too well, because it means you can spend an evening together without having to find too much to talk about, and when you come out you have the shared experience of the film to discuss. At the same time you've been close, sitting together, and ostensibly alone.

Events like concerts, football matches, races or ballet are brilliant if both parties have some reasonable amount of interest. But there is nothing worse than being dragged along to two and a half hours of something you don't like. So it is always better to try and pick something safe.

Going out for a meal together can make an excellent date although if you aren't very comfortable just chatting for a long time face to face, it could be a bit of a strain.

The best dates are not always the most exciting events. You don't really have to see Madonna live or do anything particularly extravagant. The real value from a successful night out together is the warm feelings you get from being in each other's company which could be just as good sitting in the front row at Wembley or standing at a bus stop in the rain.

Who pays?

*'I expect to have to pay and I'm worried that I won't
have enough money. If we go for a meal or get into a
club it might be really dear and I'd look stupid if I
couldn't pay.'*

Ben (16)

Money is a difficult subject to discuss at the best of times,
and I think that honesty is the best policy. If you don't think
you've got enough to cover the night's costs then say so
before or during the night. Don't wait until the end.

In this day and age hopefully there aren't many girls
who expect the bloke to pay for everything. Equally, I hope
that there are not many boys who would expect the girl to
pay for them. The main motive behind the Feminist Movement was to achieve a level of social and professional
equality between men and women. Women have striven to
be treated in the same way as men; to be paid the same
wages for doing the same work and to have an equally
strong role in terms of public and political power. So for
any male to assume that he should pay because his role is
that of the provider and earner while the female's is a
passive and less important role, is insulting. On the other
hand if one half of the party really *wants* to pay for
something then it's a kindness for the other to allow them
to do so. But when it's assumed or taken for granted that
one half will pay, then it can feel as though you're being
taken advantage of.

There are no rules, but there are precedents, for instance
people often decide to buy 'rounds'. They take it in turn to
pay for things. This means they are not continually splitting
everything down the middle, but by taking it in turns to
pay they will be more or less equal at the end of the day and
also will have shared the responsibility of providing.

What a date means and what it doesn't mean

Just because a girl agrees to go out on a date with a boy, it doesn't *mean* anything. There is a long way between going out on a date and having a relationship. Just because you've been out with someone once, it doesn't mean she's your girlfriend, or you're her boyfriend.

Any boy who assumes that he deserves good-night kisses or any other physical intimate contact because he's been out on a date with a girl is wrong. Very wrong. A date with a girl is not necessarily a prelude to anything. It is a way of getting to know someone better, and finding out whether or not you get on well.

7. What Having a Relationship Means

A relationship is about trusting, loving and respecting each other. It's not just about getting off with one another for a night and having a serious kissing session, it's about developing a friendship that involves intimacy, care, fun and honest communication. Ideally relationships are ongoing and growing, so they will continue to develop and improve as time passes, so long as both parties are willing.

'I used to wear one of my boyfriend's rugby shirts to Tech because it was his and the other girls would know I was going out with him. They would think I'd spent the night at his place too. It also made me feel good because it was like I had something of his to show off.'

Eileen (16)

Relationships are not about ownership. Being someone's girlfriend or boyfriend is not a statement or a legally binding agreement. It is only a state of mind shared between two people. What the rest of the world thinks, believes or does isn't actually an issue. What *is* an issue is how you treat each other and if you can bring each other comfort, pleasure and happiness. Those are the sort of relationships which are really worth having.

8. Being In Love

When boys do fall in love, they find it is a very powerful emotion. It has been described as follows:

'Falling in love was the happiest time in my life.'
                                                    Kevin (16)

'Falling in love is like being hit in the stomach.'
                                                  Richard (14)

'It felt nice, being wanted.'
                                                      Ian (14)

'It was like having butterflies in my stomach.'
                                                 Nicholas (13)

There were, however, a few who found it difficult to cope with such a strong emotional feeling.

'It was a hassle.'
                                                  Matthew (15)

'Love can tie you up and get you confused about things.
If you really need to concentrate for studying or work or
something it's better not to get involved.'

Christopher (16)

'Love sucks. It weakens you and makes you soft.'

Johnny (13)

For most of the boys who responded to my questionnaire,
love seems to have been a very happy experience.

But being able to feel love and being able to talk about it
are two wildly different things. A lot of boys are able to feel
it but they could never talk to their mates about what it is
that they feel, and maybe couldn't even explain it to the girl
who's actually responsible for sparking off the emotion in
the first place.

9. When It Ends

When she chucks you

One of the most painful things that any teenager has to go
through is the experience of being chucked or rejected by
someone they feel strongly about.

The fear of rejection makes asking someone out so difficult
in the first place. So, when you are eventually rejected by
someone you have gone out with, it is doubly painful. All
the same, it is important and practical to be able to deal
with rejection, as we will all have to face it in one form or
another several times through our lives.

In some ways it might seem even more difficult for boys
to cope with because they are often less able to deal with
the emotions that come up. Being chucked rocks your

confidence in yourself. It makes you feel that in some way you are not good enough because you can't have something you dearly desire.

An automatic reaction to being chucked is to cry with the hurt and to moan about the frustration. But in order to cry and moan you need the safety and security of good friends who will let you. This is a problem for boys because their friends are often too embarrassed and too closed-off to be able to cope with another boy's pain. As a result, it is considered unmanly to make a big fuss about this sort of emotional turmoil and instead you are expected to suffer in silence and solitude.

> *'If someone's been dumped then I guess it is all right to cry but only on your own in your bedroom. And it's all right to tell your mates, but the chances are they'll probably have a laugh at you.'*
>
> Kelvin (15)

Still, the most effective thing you can do is to find someone you can trust and who will respect your confidentiality; if not a friend maybe a teacher, parent, brother or sister. Tell them in detail how you feel. They can't change your situation and make it better, but if you allow yourself to admit you have all those feelings, they will eventually pass away.

If you bottle them up inside and never let them out, they might fester and turn into feelings of hate against all girls or real self-hatred, brought on by thinking that you are not good enough.

It is important to remember that rejection is just part of the process of finding the right partner. Suffering rejection doesn't mean that you're a bad person or that there's anything 'wrong' with you. All it means is that you haven't met the 'right' person yet.

Boys who learn to express themselves honestly to girls and yet also deal with any rejection will quickly learn more about themselves and relationships than boys who simply hide behind a façade. It's really only through experiencing emotions and processing them that we ever learn anything useful.

When you chuck her

When you've been in a relationship with a girl and you've cared for her and made space in your life for her, you have a duty to respect her feelings. Therefore, when you want to end that relationship or even just change its direction and intensity, it is important that you do so, taking care to cause the minimum amount of hurt.

> 'We used to go to the youth club every week. We'd meet in the hall. One week I went and he was snogging with another girl in the cloakrooms. He told me it was over and I was chucked. He told me he chucked me at the weekend. I didn't know.'
>
> *Cecilia (13)*

The most obvious policy to adopt in terms of respect for another's feelings is to put yourself in their position. How would you feel if you were treated the way you have treated your girlfriend? Can you feel confident that you've acted as honestly and as respectfully as you were able? That's the key – do unto others as you would have them do unto you.

CHAPTER FIVE
MASTURBATION

1. What Is It?

Tossing, wanking, jerking off, playing with yourself and having-one-off-the-wrist are all slang terms for the same thing: masturbation. It is the act of self-stimulation of the penis to orgasm.

Masturbation is a bit of a taboo subject, but almost everyone does it. It's one of those things which men, and indeed women, are very embarrassed about.

2. How Do You Do It?

Boys usually masturbate with their hands. The erect penis is held in the palm of the hand with the fingers wrapped gently around the shaft and the hand is moved up and down the length of the penis, moving the skin covering the penis backwards and forwards. The motion used usually starts off quite slowly and increases in speed, getting quicker as the boy gets nearer to reaching climax.

3. Climax and Ejaculation

When a boy reaches climax, if he is physically/sexually matured then he will ejaculate a whitish creamy substance called semen. Commonly known as 'spunk', the semen is the substance which carries the microscopic sperm. It's perfectly normal for semen to be lumpy sometimes and watery at others.

It's also perfectly normal to ejaculate a large amount of semen (a teaspoonful or so) or even just a tiny bubble. The amount of semen ejaculated bears absolutely no relation to its quality or fertility. Because sperm are microscopic, millions of them can be present in the tiniest bubble of fluid. And it only takes one sperm to fertilize an egg from the female's ovary.

4. Discovering Masturbation

Quite a lot of teenage boys learn how to masturbate from their friends, or from older brothers. In the innocence of early adolescence, the act of masturbation isn't regarded with any well-defined shame or embarrassment. So, as a result it is actually sometimes performed in an almost social way.

> *'Some of the boys at school have wanking competitions in the dorm or the lavatory. They see who can come the quickest and who makes the most spunk.'*
>
> *Nigel (15)*

Individually, boys may also discover how to masturbate by themselves. From a very early age (sometimes as young as 3 or 4) boys discover that if they touch and fondle their penis it will become erect. In a way, masturbation is merely an extension of this self-exploration and experimentation.

5. Mutual Masturbation

As the above quote from Nigel illustrates, it is not at all uncommon for young teenage boys to participate in mutual masturbation. This is the act whereby one boy will help another reach climax through using his hand to stimulate the other's penis.

Of course this doesn't mean you're abnormal or different if you've never encountered this experience. Not does it mean you're gay if you have. Although this is a recognized sexual practice among homosexuals, there is absolutely no evidence to suggest that boys who have been involved in mutual masturbation during their sexually-explorative teenage years grow up to become homosexual.

6. Girls and Masturbation

Girls also masturbate, by stimulating their clitoris (the pea-sized knob near the opening of the vagina) with a moist lubricated finger, again using a rhythmic movement which gradually increases in pace. And they may insert fingers or occasionally vibrators, which are usually battery operated, penis-shaped devices, into the vagina. These are designed to vibrate at a high frequency and so stimulate a girl's genital area.

'I felt guilty when I masturbated because I thought only boys needed to do it.'

Rachel (16)

There is evidence to suggest that although girls mature sexually at a younger age than boys, they are likely to masturbate less than boys in their teens. However, when they do, girls, like boys, normally use sexual fantasies, photographs and erotic passages from books to arouse and heighten their pleasure.

7. Myths of Masturbation

Even though it has a taboo reputation, there is nothing sinister, dirty or evil about masturbation. It is just the act of helping yourself to reach a sexual climax.

Masturbation causes no physical harm; it doesn't make you go blind, deaf, mad, infertile, warty, spotty, hairy-palmed, short-sighted or anything else you may have heard. If you do it often, i.e. more than twice a day, it can cause your penis to become sore and oversensitive, and it can also become a bit addictive.

> *'I think I'm addicted to masturbating. I can't stop it, I've tried to give it up but I can't, I keep touching myself and sort of get carried away.'*
>
> *Geoff (14)*

> *'Sometimes I masturbate three or four or five times a day. I make myself come looking at magazines or thinking about some of the girls at school. Sometimes I make myself sore from doing it too much or too hard.*
>
> *Steven (14)*

Masturbation, like sex, is primarily about sensual pleasure, which is a good thing, but to be excessive or over-zealous about giving youself repeated pleasure is too self-absorbing. Practised in moderation, masturbation is a wholesome exciting release. Too much is just an indulgence.

> *'Although I may occasionally masturbate now, I could never see the point when I was younger. I tried it once and didn't get anywhere. I had sex through my teens but I had no idea what an orgasm was. That didn't happen till later – when I started masturbating.'*
>
> *Christine (21)*

Masturbation can help women discover orgasms and in the same way it can help men know how to delay them.

Masturbation can help men learn how to overcome the problem of premature ejaculation (see Chapter 7 p. 77).

8. The Useful Application of Masturbation

Although there is a selfish side to masturbation, it does have its uses. By masturbating regularly, a person gets to know how they are best sexually stimulated and how they can achieve a climax in the most satisfying way. Although they may have had sex many times, some women never actually achieve an orgasm until they learn to masturbate because the clitoris is not usually stimulated during intercourse. However, with the knowledge they've learnt from masturbating of how they are most easily moved to climax, they are able to show their partner what it is they most enjoy.

For both sexes, masturbation is about pleasure and the release of sexual tension. Like all animals, we have sexual desires and urges. These may occur at times when sexual intercourse is not possible, appropriate or even desired. In these instances the simple act of masturbation provides comfort and relief.

CHAPTER SIX
BEFORE SEX

1. French Kissing

French kissing is one of those things which has developed a mythology all of its own, and one which it frankly doesn't deserve.

I receive countless letters requesting detailed information

about how you are supposed to 'do' French kissing. And lots of people write in because they are worried that they will French kiss someone 'wrongly' or 'badly' and so be the laughing stock of all their friends.

The old myth about French kissing is that it somehow carries some sort of unspoken significance or message which says 'I want to make love to you.'

Needless to say this is all just rubbish. French kissing is the name given to the type of kiss which doesn't just involve the pressing together of lips, but goes one step further and includes the touching of tongues.

Both kissers' mouths are kept slightly open during the kiss so that tongues can be mingled and each other's lips and mouths can be explored.

Because it is a more intimate and arousing method of kissing, it's obviously not the sort of kiss you'd greet your aunty with, but this doesn't mean that it signifies anything other than the fact that you enjoy that level of intimacy with whomever it is that you are kissing.

It must also be pointed out that French kissing is not necessarily very arousing or very nice, particularly the first time. It can be wet and sticky and uncomfortable, not because either party is doing it wrongly (there is no right or wrong way) but because you just don't happen to like it. Wet, tongue-filled snogs are sometimes not half as exciting as soft, sensual lip-brushing kisses. It's all a matter of personal taste.

French kissing often forms an important part of foreplay (see Chapter 7 p. 75).

2. Virginity

Virginity is not something you do, it's something you don't do. You are a virgin when you have not had sexual intercourse, yet for some reason, a lot of boys and girls are really embarrassed in their teens because they are still virgins. They view it as a really negative state which makes them stand out as different from everyone else.

But being a virgin doesn't mean you are a sexual retard. It doesn't mean you're not interested in sex and fascinated by it. All it means is that you haven't done it.

> *'Even though I am a virgin I can't stop thinking about sex. When I see good-looking women in the street who are pregnant or have children, I think about how they must have had sex. It's on my mind all the time.'*
>
> *Mike (13)*

Getting it 'out of the way'

It's as though you aren't one of the lads or one of the girls if you haven't done it. Both boys and girls have even admitted that they just randomly picked someone they knew to sleep with, simply to get it over and done with and out of the way. Some boys react to peer pressure by forcing themselves into having a sexual encounter with someone they are not emotionally or physically attracted to, which is not a good thing. Ideally sex should always involve other feelings of affection, care, consideration and desire or else it just becomes a hollow and empty act. There is really very little mileage in sex that has no emotional strings attached.

The only sensible reason to lose your virginity is in order to experience exciting, enjoyable and loving sex. But you won't honestly experience this sort of sex by having it with the first available girl you meet at a party. What you're more likely to experience is some sort of fumbling, uncaring, embarrassing event which frees you of being a 'virgin' but saddles you with a lot of disappointment and regret. (See also the chapter on sexually transmitted diseases and AIDS, pp. 11–14.)

The upshot of sex without feelings is often sadness, shame, embarrassment and a degree of self-loathing for both parties.

Lying

Boys (and to some extent girls) will lie through their teeth and pretend to their mates that they've had sex in order to keep face.

> *'When I was 15 I was still a virgin, but practically everyone else at school said they had done it. It seemed like I was the only virgin in the form. So I lied. I said I had done it with a girl on holiday. Everyone believed me, or at least no one said they didn't. They took all that I said as gospel – straight away, which makes me think that they were probably all lying too!'*
>
> John (19)

The trouble with lying is that it causes more problems than it solves. How can you show your real fears or insecurities about your first sexual encounter to your mates, when you've led everyone to believe you've already done it *ages* ago?

Virginity can actually be very positive. If you stay a virgin until you're happy that you've found the right partner, and convinced that you are both close enough to enjoy experimenting with sex together, then it's as though you're making a very important statement of trust and love.

3. Fear of Sex

One very common problem amongst teenage boys is a basic, and understandable, fear of sex. Sex becomes such a constant topic of conversation, such a wealth of mythology and such a world of expectation, that not surprisingly it is also frightening and off-putting. It is perfectly natural to be anxious about starting any form of sex life.

> *'My girlfriend wants us to have sex, she has mentioned it loads of times now and I feel her pressurizing me. I don't know if I am ready to do it. I don't know if I should tell her because she might chuck me. I'm worried that if we did do it that I wouldn't be able to satisfy her.'*
>
> *Colin (15)*

At first I was very surprised by the number of letters I received at *Just Seventeen* from boys who said they felt pressured by their girlfriend's eagerness to start sexual relations. Often it is assumed that in most teenage relationships it is the boy who is hot, randy and desperate to get to grips with sex and that the girl is constantly having to keep him at bay until she feels ready. The evidence from my letters suggests this is not true. It is, in fact, very common for the boy to feel anxious and unwilling to start having sex.

Partly this problem is caused by the fact that teenage girls achieve a higher level of physical and emotional maturity than their male counterparts, which means that they may be more keen and able to start sexual relations than boys even when they are seeing older boys. They may also be much better educated in sexual facts. The most common fears that beset teenage boys are fears of inadequacy.

An awful lot of boys are worried that they are physically ill-equipped to start a sexual relationship or are lacking in the knowledge and experience of sexual technique that they feel they *ought* to have.

'I've only got a patchy little bit of hair round my testicles and even when my penis is erect it looks smaller than most of the other lads' do when they're just soft and normal. What do I do if she laughs at me or tells everyone that I can't do it?'

Kevin (14)

A certain amount of fear and apprehension about sex is actually quite a constructive thing in boys. At least it causes them to think; to investigate and examine their role and their desires in a sexual relationship, rather than just plunging head-first, unprepared into the world of sex. It may hopefully allow them time and space to consider what is realistically involved. It also affords them a chance to think with their head and not just act with their groin.

4. Sex at Sixteen

The law in Britain decrees that it is illegal for either boys or girls to participate in sexual intercourse with a member of the opposite sex under the age of 16 and for males to participate in intercourse with members of the same sex under the age of 21. This is called the age of consent. So for a boy of any age to have sex with a girl who is under 16 is a serious criminal offence which may be punished by anything ranging from probation to a custodial sentence.

This law was created to protect young people. Although a lot of teenagers may feel that the age is set too high and is oppressively limiting to their desires, it wasn't designed that way.

Without doubt there are a great many boys and girls who are physically and mentally mature enough to start having sex younger than 16. Similarly there are many who at 16 are still too immature to become involved in sexual activity.

What the law has done is to decide on a reasonable age above which it can be assumed that a *majority* of young people will be sufficiently equipped both in essential knowledge and physical maturity to partake of sex.

Having said that, my postbag every week is crammed full of letters from readers who have started having sex younger than the age of consent. It would be stupid for me or any other problem page writer to pretend that it wasn't happening and it wouldn't be reasonable just to keep quoting chapter and verse of the law which states that you shouldn't have sex under 16.

What we can do is to try and provide everyone with as much practical knowledge and self-respect as possible to help them understand what sex involves, what the risks are and what are the right and wrong reasons for doing it.

5. Boys' Sexual Fantasies

Fantasies are daydreams, and for teenagers, they are almost always sexual. One pleasure of fantasies is that they are just that – fantasies. They are not acted on, they will rarely be fulfilled but they are very pleasant. What do teenage boys really fantasize about?

The questionnaire provided some illuminating answers:

> *'My big fantasy is to be playing my favourite sport, football, and to be scoring an unassisted goal while my girlfriend is watching.'*
>
> *David (14)*

'Having an orgy.'

Callum (13)

'Being with Kim Bassinger.'

Matthew (15)

'Having sex with a girl in a field of wet grass.'

Tony (18)

'Being a big star like Tom Cruise.'

Jason (15)

'I imagine I am with my friend Tony's mum and she is doing things to me or I'm with the art teacher at school.'

David (14)

CHAPTER SEVEN
THE SEXUAL ACT

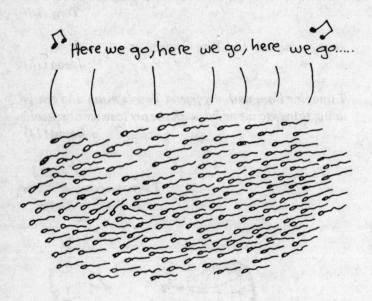

♪ Here we go, here we go, here we go.....

1. Sex for the First Time

'The first time I ever did it it was a complete disaster. Rachel and I had been going out for a few months and we'd planned it. We knew it was going to happen on this particular night at a friend's party. But I got really drunk. I can't quite remember exactly what happened but I know it was a disaster and it was all over very quickly.'

Mark (20)

A lot of men have admitted to me that they were unable to tell the truth about their first sexual experiences until years later. At the time when it actually occurred, even those who suffered from nerves, premature ejaculation, guilt, anxiety, worry, shame and embarrassment, or else could only vaguely picture the half-remembered scene experienced through a thick alcoholic haze, still boasted to their mates about what a brilliant time they had.

Boys say they needed to brag about their first time because it was hard enough to admit to themselves, let alone to another male, the feelings of disillusionment and disappointment which they really experienced.

Girls often have the same sort of experience.

'It was all very fumbled and very quick. I can remember as soon as it was over all I wanted to do was go and tell my mates I'd done it. That was the first thing on my mind, the fact that I could say I really had done it. But at the same time I was thinking – is that it? Is that what all the fuss is about?

Stephanie (17)

2. Problems Encountered

First time sex can be a very harrowing and traumatic experience for boys. And often they are not able to cope with any strong emotions that are brought up, due to their comparative emotional immaturity and the fact that they aren't encouraged to share their feelings easily with their mates.

Because being able to 'perform' sexually carries such a ridiculous weight of macho stigma, there is a lot of pressure and anticipation brought to bear on the first sexual encounter.

Yet, the very first time you have sex, either for a boy or a girl, it is likely to be the most difficult. It's a bit like jumping into a car for the very first time in your life and expecting to be able to drive it away perfectly, made worse only by the fact that all your mates are standing around watching you.

Even for men and women who have had a few sexual partners and many experiences of sex, the first time they sleep with someone new it is always tricky and complicated just getting used to each other. So, expecting your very first time with *anyone* to be easy is daft. First time sex is *not* easy.

The practical problems which may affect boys can include:

1) Having difficulty exciting and stimulating your partner before penetration.
2) Getting and maintaining an erection.
3) Finding a mutually comfortable and suitable position to offer easy entry for the penis into the vagina.
4) Avoiding becoming over-excited and over-stimulated and so suffering from premature ejaculation (coming too quickly).
5) Being able to excite and satisfy your partner during sex so that she too finds the experience rewarding.
6) Protection against sexually transmitted diseases and AIDS.

3. Solving the Problems

There are certain good books which are dedicated to graphically explaining sexual technique and practices which are listed in the bibliography section on page 109, but *Boys About Boys* is not intended to be a sex manual so this book won't go into any great detail.

However, with a little correct knowledge and a sensible

approach it is possible to avoid and overcome the common obstacles that I've mentioned.

Foreplay

Foreplay is the name given to the intimate touching and kissing that should occur before any penetration of the vagina takes place or before you commence sexual intercourse.

One way of viewing foreplay is as scene-setting. Instead of going from normal, everyday life, straight into active, physical sex, it is important to gradually set the mood so that both of you can begin to feel relaxed, intimate and aroused. For this reason, especially when attempting to have first-time sex, it's really far better to be somewhere comfortable, warm and secure where there is no risk of interruption.

Kissing, hugging, cuddling, stroking, caressing, rubbing, nibbling, licking and speaking softly are all a part of foreplay. Any intimate, considerate and caring physical contact made immediately before sexual intercourse is part of foreplay.

Similarly by caressing her breasts and sucking or stroking her nipples you can gradually and gently help her to relax and become sexually stimulated.

Then, when a girl begins to feel sexually aroused, her vagina will become moist and warm. This is an indication of her level of excitement, as well as being the body's natural mechanism to make penetration easier.

A more specific example of foreplay though includes clitoral stimulation. The clitoris is a small pea-sized knob of flesh which lies near the opening of a girl's vagina, and gently rubbing and caressing this with your finger will help arouse and stimulate your partner. Indeed, continued foreplay in the form of clitoral stimulation is often essential for some women to achieve a full orgasm. Most women are able to come from just having their clitoris gently and rhythmically rubbed and fondled, whereas not that many women are able to come just from being penetrated by a man's penis, if it is not preceded or followed by some clitoral stimulation. This has to do with the fact that the clitoris doesn't receive that much physical contact during conventional penetrative sex.

Penetration of the vagina by the penis is by no means the only way that a man and a woman can achieve sexual satisfaction. Apart from just being a gentle prelude to sex, foreplay can substitute for penetrative sex and be just as exciting and satisfying.

So much is foreplay and general caressing the key to successful sex, that even if you do find yourself occasionally troubled by the problems mentioned, happiness and sexual satisfaction can still be achieved by lots of warmth and touching. Good sex is not about how big, how hard or how long the penis is, or how athletic your performance is. It's about how much you care and understand.

> *'The actual sex bit was no big deal, it was over quite quickly anyway. What made it all so brilliant was the closeness and the warmth and the fact that we were alone together all night.'*
>
> Marina (18)

Finding the right position

There is a myth that the more bizarre and gymnastic the position the greater lover you are and consequently girls will be thrilled by your performance. This, like most myths, is utter undiluted rubbish.

It's true that there are a whole variety of weird and wonderful positions which may be employed, whereby the penis can achieve entry to the vagina. Initially, anyway, the traditional 'missionary' position, where the girl lies on her back and the man lies between her legs, is probably the preferable way to have sex for the first time. Apart from anything else it means that the couple are able to face one another to kiss, hug, hold and to look into each other's eyes.

It is much more important to try and make first-time sex as comfortable and as close as possible and not to turn it into some sort of gymnastic obstacle course.

Curing premature ejaculation and lack of erection

Premature ejaculation is when a man comes too quickly during intercourse and is therefore unable to have what could be a slow, sensual sexual experience. Masturbation can be a useful tool to avoid this, either by making yourself come once before intercourse, and so releasing the excitement and tension and therefore allowing the second erection to last longer. Or else merely by practising control of the orgasm by holding back while masturbating.

Just as premature ejaculation is caused by nervousness and over-excitement, so is not being able to get or maintain an erection. If you are normally able to achieve an erection and masturbate to climax without problems, then almost certainly the only problem is the pressure and worry that naturally arises when you first start having sex.

For both these physical problems foreplay is a useful and comforting alternative.

4. Sharing Your Sexual Experiences

With your girlfriend

The more able you are to talk with your partner, the more satisfying your sex will become. Being able to discuss your fears and worries and slowly work through any problems that arise together is the key to a healthy sexual relationship, because both of you are involved and communicating with each other.

If sex is just something you both do in the dark, and never discuss, it is impossible to find out how the other feels about it and for it to improve and develop.

Men and women of all ages have a block about discussing sex, as they find it embarrassing. But sharing intimately with your partner can be fun, can be exciting, and best of all it can lead to knowledge and better, more fulfilling sexual experiences.

> *'The first time it happened I was devastated. It was like I was finished before I'd started. I just wanted to get up and run away. I was really angry at myself for being so useless. But, when it happened again, Dawn said it didn't matter and asked me what it felt like. We ended up talking and even having a bit of a laugh. Now if it happens we'll just muck about and kiss and that, then try again later.'*
>
> *Chris (18)*

With your mates

'Duncan used to sit at the back of the bus on Monday morning and tell us exactly what he'd done with his bird on Saturday night. He'd tell us everything: where

he put his hands, if they'd done it, where, what her minge looked like . . . everything.'

Warren (16)

What you and your partner get up to in bed is something very close and personal between the two of you and shouldn't be bragged about.

There's a very big difference between bragging about sexual experiences and sharing fears and feelings honestly. All too often when boys talk about sex to one another, it usually turns out to be a catalogue of lies about how many times they did what, where and with whom. And this sort of talk is useless. If everybody lied about sex, pretended to be doing it, or enjoying it, when they weren't, nobody would be able to learn from each other. All we end up knowing is a pack of stud fairy tales which are no good to man or beast.

It seems that girls find it easier to talk honestly about the emotions that surround sex and are less concerned about their performance, and have a greater ability to consider sex not just as a physical act, but as a more complex, involved experience.

I'm not suggesting for one moment that groups of boys should sit together at the back of the school bus and discuss their feelings about sex. This wouldn't work (at least I don't think it would). But if you have one good friend you can talk to intimately, and most of all *honestly*, then, if you share your experiences and impressions, you are much more likely to develop a clear, realistic picture of sex in a few close conversations than in a whole lifetime of earwigging on silly macho boys' talk.

5. Six Boys' Experiences of Sex

Here are a few quotes from boys which illustrate some of
the common experiences which happen to boys who have
decided to start having sex. They help to paint a picture of
what sex is really about and give an idea of some of the
things you need to know, and should be able to come to
terms with.

*'I think there is something wrong with me. I haven't
had sex very many times, but every time I do, it is over
really quickly, sometimes it's only seconds. But when I
am masturbating it lasts a lot longer.'*

Ben (15)

*'Even when we'd both agreed we'd do it and we had her
house all to ourselves, it still didn't happen. I just
couldn't get my penis to go inside her. I couldn't seem
to get the angle right or find the opening.'*

Neil (17)

*'I can tell my girlfriend was really disappointed with
sex with me. She's never actually said anything. I know
she's never had an orgasm and I don't have a clue what
I should do.'*

Aaron (16)

*'For ages all I wanted was just to do it. I didn't really
care who with, just someone who would let me. The first
time I did was behind a garage standing up. Neither of
us really took our clothes off and when it was over I
didn't feel that good. I felt a bit sick really and just
wanted to get away.'*

Nick (17)

'Since we have been having sex I can't handle her having other boyfriends. I know she does and it makes me feel mad and sick inside. When I think of them doing it to her I go mad.'

Mick (18)

'I'd been going out with Kath for three and a half months before we had proper sex. I was a virgin but she wasn't. She'd only done it with one bloke before me but she said she'd had a really bad time. I wanted it to be right and I was a bit scared it wouldn't be OK. In the end when we did it it was all a bit of a laugh really. Dead good though.'

Alex (17)

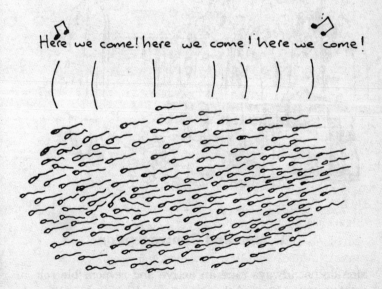

CHAPTER EIGHT
CONTRACEPTION

1. Men and Contraception

Men do not always take an active and responsible role in contraception. Instead they've often relied on the woman to choose the method of contraception, to supply it and to initiate its use.

This is due partly to ignorance in not fully understanding what all the contraceptive alternatives are, and partly to the fact that, for some couples, sex just happens and is not talked about, so methods of contraception are never discussed. But perhaps most of all, there is a certain attitude which has ingrained itself into the male mind that shirks any responsibility, because it is felt that birth control is up to the female.

If a male says, 'Contraception has nothing to do with me' he is deluding himself. Assuming that he wouldn't be cowardly enough to shirk responsibility, he would have to deal with problems of unwanted pregnancy too.

'It's girls that get pregnant so it's up to them to deal with contraceptives. It's their look-out and it's them that'll get into trouble. Men shouldn't have to do anything.'

Nathan (15)

This sort of attitude is unfair to women, because not only does it lumber them with doing all the work and planning, it also saddles them with the burden of coping with unwanted pregnancy alone. Men lose out too, in terms of missing another important facet of a relationship which can actually help to bring two people closer.

Contraception can provide a couple with another means of caring and sharing. If a man takes no responsibility he's cutting himself off from yet another area of experience and he's closing the door on an important aspect of his partner's life.

In a recent interview with a group of teenage boys, I was encouraged to discover that the all too real risk of AIDS had caused a high percentage of the boys to become aware of condoms and consider them a useful addition to their sex lives.

It is a fact that condoms, if used correctly, can greatly reduce any chances of the HIV virus being transmitted between sexual partners. And it was reassuring to hear that the boys had taken serious note of this and were willing to use them in order to 'protect themselves'.

What was a bit daunting, though, was that they didn't really consider them as contraceptives, or rather they were only interested in what condoms could do for *them*. The fact that they could also enormously reduce the risk of unwanted pregnancy was not important. They were concerned that they didn't get AIDS, but they didn't seem concerned about the prospects of pregnancy. That still remained the 'girl's business'.

2. Different Methods

There are currently nine recognized methods of contraception. It is important to realize that all methods are only as reliable as the person using them.

(i) The pill

The pill is one of the most popular methods used in Britain today. If it is taken correctly it can be over 99% effective. The combined pill contains two artificial hormones, oestrogen and progestogen. Oestrogen prevents the eggs from being released, and progestogen creates a mucus which plugs the entrance to the womb and makes the womb lining unlikely to accept an egg. There are many different brands, with different amounts of hormones in them. This pill is taken regularly either for 21 days, with a break of 7 days in between packs during which time there will be some breakthrough bleeding, or for 28 days – the ED or Everyday Pill. The mini-pill if taken correctly is 98% effective. The mini-pill contains only the hormone progestogen. The important thing to remember about the mini-pill is that it has to be taken at exactly the same time every day.

The advantage of the pill is that it is easy to use. It also helps with period problems, such as PMT and heavy periods, and protects against cancer of the ovary and uterus (womb). The disadvantages are that it can have some complicated side-effects, including a possible link with some cancers, including breast, cervix and liver.

(ii) The condom

The condom is, if used correctly (use only a condom with the BSI Kitemark on the packet), up to 98% effective. The advantages are that it is cheap, readily available, easy to use and free from family planning clinics. It is the one contraceptive which men are mainly responsible for. The condom helps protect both partners against HIV, the virus that leads to AIDS and other STDs (sexually transmitted diseases). It may also protect the woman against cancer of the cervix.

A condom protects against the HIV virus and other sexually transmitted diseases by creating a barrier between the sexual organs. This barrier stops either semen, vaginal fluids, menstrual or other blood from being exchanged between partners. If no fluids are exchanged then the risk of virus transfer is eliminated.

But, of course, to create an effective barrier the condom has to be used correctly. First, the condom has to be fitted on to the penis before any genital contact is made. This is because there is often pre-come semen present at the tip of an erect penis. This pre-ejaculation ejaculation occurs perfectly naturally when the male is aroused, and it may not only contain millions of fertile sperm which could cause pregnancy, but can also contain the HIV virus if the male is a carrier.

The condom *must* be used properly. It has also been shown that up to 2% of all condoms may split, usually because they are put on wrongly. So an added precaution that may be used is to employ the condom in conjunction with a cap (diaphragm, see below) and/or spermicide cream. The theory being that if any semen escape through the condom, they will be killed off by the cream.

If the condom doesn't split, it will do a great job of stopping the virus on its own. If you take into account that the HIV virus is something like 30 times smaller than a single sperm, the effect of the virus getting through a waterproof condom is equivalent to it forcing its way through 3000 feet of rubber.

But, after using the condom, it's also important that it is removed very soon after ejaculation. The penis must be withdrawn from the vagina and the condom removed before the penis is allowed to become limp or else there is a risk that semen will squeeze out of the loosening neck of the condom.

Every packet of condoms includes clear instructions on how they should be used, these should be read carefully and followed. Condoms are an essential part of safer penetrative sex, but only if used properly.

(iii) The diaphragm

The diaphragm or cap is up to 97% effective. It is a small rubber circular cover which the female fits over her cervix (the entrance to her womb) prior to sexual intercourse. It is a safe and simple form of contraception used in conjunction with spermicide jelly, but must be professionally fitted for the first time, which requires the woman to attend a clinic and be told how to use it.

(iv) The coil

The coil or IUD (intra-uterine device) unlike the cap is a semi-permanent type of contraception which is up to 99% effective. It is a device made out of either plastic or copper which is fitted by a doctor inside a female's cervix. It works by stopping the egg from settling in the womb and preventing the egg and sperm 'meeting'. It is not generally fitted to women until they have had at least one or more children. Some women do develop a pelvic infection, and there are other rare complications.

(v) The sponge

The sponge is a small foam sponge which is 91% effective. It is impregnated with spermicide (a chemical which kills sperm) and it can easily be inserted into the vagina. However it is not the most effective form of contraception and is comparatively expensive if used regularly.

(vi) The natural method

The natural or rhythm method, which is up to 93% effective, is a method which aims to determine the days in the month when a woman is likely to become pregnant. This is done by determining when a woman will ovulate (be fertile), through counting the days in the month and taking body temperature. A practised person can estimate when is the safe time to have sex. It is a complex and involved system which requires planning and a level of expertise. It is definitely not suitable in a new relationship.

(vii) Injectable contraceptives

Injectable contraceptives are up to 99% effective. They are injections of chemicals which stop the egg from being released. They are not in common use in this country at present and are not always available. They should be used only as a last choice method.

(viii) Sterilization

Sterilization is a permanent surgical method of contraception which for women means an operation to have the fallopian tubes which carry the egg closed off. For men the operation, called vasectomy, involves cutting the tubes which carry the sperm to the penis. Obviously the permanence of this method makes it unsuitable for any young person.

(ix) The morning-after pill

If you have unprotected sex or your method of contraception fails (for example, the condom bursts) this pill can be taken by the woman up to 72 hours afterwards. It is unpleasant to take and not good for the body, so it should be regarded as 'emergency' contraception.

There are more methods of contraception being researched and developed all the time. And there are plenty of books, some of which are mentioned in the back of this book, that go into greater depth and detail over the individual methods and their specific advantages.

3. Popular Myths About Contraception

Here's a list of the most popular myths that have been circulated about contraception:

None of these statements is true:

1) *'If a boy withdraws his penis before he comes, then the girl won't get pregnant.'*

Phillip (16)

2) *'If you have sex when you're drunk, then your sperm is much weaker and won't make her pregnant.'*

Sean (15)

3) *'If the girl has a shower or a bath after and washes the spunk out then it's OK.'*

Kevin (14)

4) *'When she's having her period then you don't have to use anything because she can't get pregnant.'*

Nick (14)

5) *'It's impossible to get pregnant the first time you have sex if you're a girl.'*

Stephen (14)

6) *'Making love standing up means it's much harder for the sperm to get near and fertilize her.'*

Sean (15)

7) *'When a guy makes love for the second time in one night, his sperm isn't active any more.'*

Garth (18)

8) *'No pubic hair means you're not at puberty so you wouldn't be able to get a girl into trouble.'*

Danny (13)

9) *'If a girl's got a tampon inside her vagina when she has sex it will soak up all the sperm fluid.'*

Chris (16)

10) *'A girl has to come to get pregnant. If she doesn't come then she won't get pregnant.'*

Stuart (14)

11) *'There's no way a girl can get pregnant unless she has proper sex.'*

Tyrone (16)

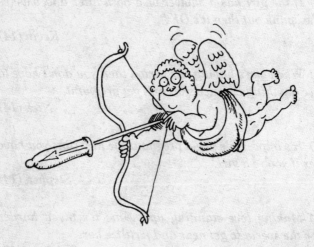

CHAPTER NINE
HOMOSEXUALITY

1. What Is a Homosexual?

The common definition of a homosexual is someone who is sexually attracted to members of the same sex. So a man who fancies other men is a homosexual and often referred to as 'gay'. Likewise a woman who is turned on by other women is also a homosexual or a 'lesbian'.

There are other terms used to describe male homosexuals and these are often used in an insulting and derogatory way. The most common of these include 'poof', 'pansy' and 'queer'. For lesbians the most usual term of insult is 'dyke'.

Homosexuals are often picked on as underdogs, partly because they deviate from what the majority feel is right or good or 'normal', but also because they are themselves a minority.

However, one in ten people, both men and women are homosexual. So in Britain alone there are over six million gays.

But sexuality, whether it is homosexuality or the more usual heterosexuality (the attraction of men to women and vice versa) is rarely straightforward and clean-cut. Most men and women who would call themselves heterosexuals will have had some sort of homosexual experience at some time in their lives. This experience can take the form of anything from an adolescent crush or a quick snog to having full sexual intercourse.

There are men who have been married and have fathered children who would still state that they are essentially homosexual. And there are homosexuals who choose occasionally to sleep with women, just as there are lesbians who will sleep with men. In fact, there are few people who are truly 100% homosexual or 100% heterosexual.

Our sexuality is not necessarily finite and fixed from birth. On the contrary it is something which grows and develops throughout the passage of our lives.

2. Adolescent Confusion and Fantasies

The early to mid teens is the period when most people start to become sexually aware as this is when the body begins to develop sexually. But it can be a time of great confusion and worry for many, as they are unsure as to the direction their sexuality is taking.

> *'When I'm in the showers after PE I sometimes get erections when I see other boys getting washed. I can't understand it. I can't make myself fancy girls, I've tried and I just feel funny when I'm with other boys. Is there some kind of drug or therapy I can take? Will I be gay for the rest of my life?'*
>
> *Paul (15)*

This sort of confusion is very common in both girls and boys during adolescence. To be sexually aroused by a member of your own sex, especially during something as intimate as showering together, is really no big deal, and is definitely not a sure indication of your sexuality. Nor is having a crush or experiencing feelings of love and admiration for a friend.

If you can imagine, your body is only just developing the mechanisms of sexual arousal and awareness so it hasn't become particularly discerning. Any form of sexual stimulus or physical intimacy could easily trigger an erection for a boy. But it doesn't actually mean very much and it certainly doesn't indicate any sexual preference. It's just a few random impulses reacting automatically and without your control to the intimacy of the situation.

Homosexual fantasies are something else which cause a lot of boys untold confusion and grief but are very common

in the teenage years. The example of having an erection in
the showers is a very common situation where your penis
seems to have a life of its own and will behave and perform
without your conscious consent. In the same way, the mind
can play tricks with you when it comes to sexual, masturbating fantasies.

> 'At night in my dorm I masturbate thinking about a
> boy in my House. This particularly turns me on. But I
> don't want to be gay and I hope this is just a phase I'm
> going through.'
>
> *Simon (14)*

Sexual fantasies are just fantasies. They don't necessarily
bear any relation to reality. Having a masturbation fantasy
about a friend doesn't mean that you want to have sex with
him. You might just be short of stimulating messages to focus
on when you're trying to reach a climax. Especially in a case
like this, where a boy attends an all-male boarding school,
he may just not have experienced enough female company
to be able to conjure up any suitable sexy scenarios.

There is also a lot of fantasy mileage in the fact that
homosexual sex has such a taboo image, which can in itself
make the prospect seem naughty and exciting, and therefore
sexually stimulating, during masturbation. Again, this
doesn't necessarily mean that the teenage fantasizer is a
closet homosexual, it just illustrates the lengths to which
their imagination will go in order to create excitement.

3. Am I Gay?

Time and time again I read letters from boys expressing a
fear of homosexuality. There is a strong misconception

among young men that homosexuality is something which is contagious, something which you'll catch if you're not careful. And there is another train of thought which believes that you can be *made* into a homosexual by being forced to wear girlie-type clothes when you're a baby. There are even those who worry that being gay is a sexual state which is hereditary and therefore can be passed down from father to son.

> *'My father went to live with another man and I feel as though I am following in my dad's footsteps because I think I'm in love with a male teacher. Is gayness hereditary? I recently stayed at my dad's and I'm worried that I might have caught AIDS off the cutlery.'*
>
> Graham (17)

The fear and negativity with which a lot of men regard homosexuality is caused by a complex state of affairs. There are some obvious reasons why certain macho heterosexuals are aggressively anti-gay and others which are not so obvious.

4. Homophobia

> *'I don't really care what gays get up to when they're on their own, so long as they don't try anything on with me. And I definitely don't mix with any of them, because I don't want anybody thinking I might be gay. You see, not everyone shares my level of acceptance.'*
>
> Russell (16)

There is a term known as homophobia, which means an irrational fear and hatred of homosexuals. Sadly, this hate is often expressed violently in disgusting 'queer-bashing' attacks or in the form of verbal abuse by men who claim that homosexuals ought to be punished for what they practise.

Quite often this violent tendency and irrational hatred is a strange sort of cover-up in some men to disguise their own hidden feelings. There are certain male and certain female characteristics in everybody. It is important to have a good balance of both male and female characteristics in order to achieve a healthy personality. But, of course, there are a lot of very macho men who don't want to recognize that they have certain kinder, more sensitive aspects to their character make-up. To them it's not considered cool to be aware of any femininity in themselves. And, more to the point, they don't want to be put in touch with any underlying part of themselves that might have very natural and normal homosexual tendencies and feelings. This, in their opinion, would definitely blow their credibility.

So, in that respect, a lot of males respond with overt aggression towards homosexuality because they feel threatened (either consciously or unconsciously) that their own confused sexuality might be exposed. It's like they have to act double tough in case someone might otherwise detect a note of softness in them.

Homophobia has increased with the advent of AIDS. Unscrupulous newspapers started referring to AIDS as the 'gay plague' because the homosexual community of San Francisco was the first large group in the West to be identified as suffering from the disease. We now know that homosexuals and heterosexuals alike are equally vulnerable to the HIV virus which can lead to AIDS.

There are, however, certain lifestyles and certain sections of the community who are most likely to contract the virus owing to their behaviour. Drug addicts who inject are more at risk if they share syringes with other users; very actively promiscuous people who have a large number of sexual partners, and homosexuals through having unprotected anal sex, are at risk.

In these examples though, people are not at risk because of what they *are*, either an addict or gay; they are at risk because of how they choose to behave. A heroin addict who always uses clean needles or a gay who has one faithful partner are not necessarily putting themselves at risk.

5. Glad To Be Gay

'It took me a lot of time and courage to tell my mother I was gay. My mother was very shocked at first, but she did get used to it. And she now accepts it. I have since moved in with someone and now we are living together. We are happy. In fact I think I'm the happiest I've ever been in my life'.

Stephan (20)

A person's sexuality is such a fundamental part of who they are that it can cause them a great deal of misery and loneliness when they deny to themselves what they really feel. A lot of boys who write to me expressing that they are gay, do so with such conviction and self-knowledge that it is hard to deny that they know what their sexuality really is. But even that strong conviction is sometimes not enough to let them find the courage to admit to the world that they are gay.

'I'm 16 and I'm gay. I know that I'm gay. But I feel so alone. I think that if someone found out that I'm gay

they would reject me. All I want is someone to hold, to be with and share my feelings.'

David (16)

Not surprisingly, in the light of such things as homophobia and 'queer-bashing', some gays, both men and women, are afraid to 'come out', to admit that they are homosexual, because they are afraid of hostility and rejection.

There are now a great many gay societies, self-help groups and telephone lines available all over the country. These can offer advice, information and friendship to young people who are unsure about how to express their sexuality, if they express it at all.

Every person's circumstances and situations are different, so there is no right or wrong way to 'come out'. A great deal can obviously be learnt from talking to other gay people who have been through the same experiences.

The most important thing is to achieve a comfortable and happy lifestyle that suits you. The worst thing has to be living a lie; where you are constantly denying the way you really feel by behaving in a manner that contradicts it. Keeping your real feelings hidden away as dark secrets is not a healthy way to live.

Being able to talk to someone who you feel you can trust and honestly open up to, whether they be a family member, a close friend or someone you've met through a society, is the first step. Admitting feelings that have for so long remained unspoken can create such a welcome sense of release.

A lot of gays will point out that when they did actually decide to admit to their sexuality, it was like having a weight suddenly lifted off their shoulders. They discovered an identity that they could share with other men in the same situation and rather than feeling rejection, for the first time they actually felt that they belonged.

There are undoubtedly many difficulties concerned with being homosexual. But then, exactly the same could be said of heterosexuality. Homosexuals and heterosexuals want the same thing, to meet a partner whose company and intimacy brings happiness. Being gay just suggests that your means to the same end is different. We all basically just want to love and be loved. Homosexuals seek this enviable state through relationships with their own sex, whereas heterosexuals choose members of the opposite sex.

We all have a responsibility to achieve our own happiness as best we can.

6. Bisexuality

A person who is bisexual is someone who can enjoy sexual relations with either sex. They may be predominantly homosexual but choose to occasionally sleep with a member of the opposite sex, predominantly heterosexual but occasionally sleep with someone of the same sex, or indeed someone who does not particularly discriminate between having sex with either gender and finds them both equally rewarding.

Like both heterosexuality and homosexuality, bisexuality is a normal and natural state; some would argue that it is the *most* natural sexuality because it explores the male and female facets that exist in everybody's character.

Rather than seeing it as a state of confusion or indecision, bisexuals look upon their sexuality as a positive state because in their eyes they are able to get the best of both worlds.

7. Homosexual Love-making

Homosexual men enjoy the same sexual moves with each other as heterosexual men do with women. They will kiss, hug, stroke, cuddle, caress, lick and fondle each other with the same fondness and passion that heterosexuals do.

Like heterosexuals, homosexuals may also have oral sex with each other, and they may, but by no means always, partake of anal sex too. Anal sex is like vaginal sex except that the anus as opposed to the vagina is penetrated by the penis. Anal sex is by no means a prerequisite of homosexuality. Indeed, not all homosexuals participate in any form of penetrative sex whatsoever, but might instead be completely content with just having intimate physical and mental closeness in a relationship.

It is actually illegal for anyone under the age of 21 to indulge in anal sex, because the law in this country states that this should be the age of consent for practising homosexuals.

Although it may sound daft, sex is really only a very small part of a person's sexuality, especially in the 1990s when blatant promiscuous sex is impractical and potentially fatal due to AIDS. Sex is actually quite secondary. Often what people seek most is comfort, company and affection.

It is all too easy to be lonely, no matter what your sexuality.

CHAPTER TEN
WHAT GIRLS WANT TO KNOW ABOUT BOYS

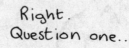

In the questionnaire that I prepared to gather information from boys for this book, I included just one question which was addressed specifically to girls: *What would you most like to know about boys?*

In the following section I've collected a selection of answers to this question which invariably take the form of questions themselves. Questions which on consideration give an insight into the image some boys present to girls, and how girls interpret that image. The answers fell into three distinct categories or areas of enquiry: Friendships, Relationships and Sex.

Many of the answers to the questions have already been provided in the preceding pages. Those that have not, I have tried to give here.

1. Friendships

'How do boys cope with having their macho image when they are depressed? And why can't they talk to their best mate and have a good cry? If they ever did would it just make them feel stupid and weak?'

Rachel (13)

'Why do they pretend to be hard all the time?'

Kath (13)

'Why do some boys think they look big to their friends when they're drinking alcohol when really they make themselves look small and can't hold it?'

Stephanie (14)

'How much of the things they say to each other are true?'

Frances (12)

'Why do they have to show off in front of their friends?'
                                                    Lucy (13)

'Why do they call you names, even when they know they like you?'
                                                    Carol (14)

What comes across from all these questions is the strange 'friendships' which boys have with each other. Girls must feel that it is difficult to have true friendships or relationships with boys, as boys don't seem able to have proper friendships with their mates.

2. Relationships

'What do they look for in a relationship and do they think that it is the boys who should start a relationship?'
                                                    Nina (16)

'Would they be put off a relationship if the girl didn't want a sexual relationship?'
                                                    Kim (15)

'When a boy is making moves at you and you start responding they go all shy and then stop. But if you don't respond they say you are frigid – why?'
                                                    Lauren (15)

'Would they go out with girls who had the personality but not the looks or a good body?'
                                                    Tasmin (14)

*'Why do they go out with girls for one thing, love them
and leave them and use them, just to be a complete
bastard really?'*

Sara (16)

'Why do they get so jealous and possessive?'

Fiona (14)

*'Why do most blokes think about sex and nothing else?
Why do they expect you to jump straight into bed with
them?'*

Leila (15)

'Do they really love you or do they just say it?'

Carole (13)

'How do you know when he's going to dump you?'

Paula (12)

The lasting impression that I get is that girls expect there
to be straightforward answers to these questions and they
assume boys know the answers, and forget that the answers
to many of the questions would vary considerably from boy
to boy.

However some of them are more answerable than others.
For instance, there still exists the outmoded concept that
boys should make the first move. But once girls realize that
boys are often as unsure of themselves as girls are, they
may be more confident in making a move.

A lot of boys would be flattered and relieved if the girl
took some control of the dating situation.

3. Sex

*'Why do boys feel they have to have a marvellous sex life
and brag about the things they do with their girlfriends
to their mates. And why do they do a lot of horrible
things to girls just to impress their mates?'*

Coral (16)

'Why are they scared to admit that they are virgins?'
Tasmin (15)

'Are older boys more likely to want sex on the first date?'
Lucy (15)

'Do they think it's their fault if a woman gets pregnant?'
Claire (14)

'Would a boy want to have sex with an overweight girl?'
Imogen (16)

'Why do they have to masturbate?'

Emma (15)

'What does fingering a girl do for a boy?'
Carmel (14)

'What do boys fantasize about?'

Mary (14)

Once again, I can't help feeling when I read through the
questions these girls have asked, that somehow they feel
that boys have the upper hand and are in charge of the
situation.

This is not the case, and certainly *should* not be the case.

Which brings me to my final question: Do you want to go out with me on friday night?

No one should ever have sex because they feel they ought to and no one should succumb to any pressure to have sex.

When boys are playing their sexual-conquests-to-impress-the-lads type of games, they should be avoided at all costs because any relations with them will only lead to grief.

Just because boys start investigating their own personal sex life earlier (i.e. they generally start masturbating younger than girls), this doesn't mean they are more sexually mature. Far from it. The most important and fulfilling aspects of any sexual relationship are the emotions and feelings that accompany it and these are what require maturity and sensitivity; two things which a lot of teenage boys are often sadly lacking.

Do boys just regard sex as some sort of conquest which once they have achieved they will then go and brag to their mates about? Or do they actually have any real and honest feelings of care and affection about the girl they are having sex with?

The general opinion is that boys are more interested in the physical side of a relationship while girls are more interested in the emotional side.

Maybe this fits in with the theory that boys don't think about things, so much as just reacting to situations and pressures.

BIBLIOGRAPHY

Belfield, Toni and Martins, Helen
Introduction to Family Planning. FPIS 60 pence.
Explains how each method of contraception works, reliability, who it suits, ease of use and how family planning can become part of general health.

Bruggen, Peter and O'Brian, Charles
Surviving Adolescence. Faber & Faber £3.95.
A handbook for adolescents and their parents.

Butterworth, Jane
Straight Talk: How to Handle Sex. Pan £4.50 (pub. September 1993).
An invaluable and comprehensive guide to sex.

Cox, Gill and Damow, Sheila
Making the Most of Loving. Sheldon Press £4.99.

Greenwood, Judy
Personal Relationships. Chambers £2.25.
Discusses relationships in the community, at work, with family and sexual relationships, for teenagers.

Harper, Anita
Love Hurts: Young Love and Its Problems. Piccadilly Press £8.95.

Harris, Thomas
I'm OK, You're OK. Pan £5.99.
Bestseller aims to help gain control of yourself, your

relationships and your future – 'no matter what has happened in the past'.

Kreitman, Tricia
Making It – How To Handle Love. Pan £3.50 (pub. April 1993).
Everything you need to know about love and sex, from falling in and out of love to maintaining a warm and loving relationship.

Mayle, Peter
What's Happening To Me? Macmillan £6.99.
Illustrated guide to puberty presented with humour.

Metcalf, Andy and Humphries, Martin (editors)
The Sexuality of Men. Pluto Press £4.95.
Ten men explore male attitudes.

Claire Patterson
It's OK to be You!
– Feeling Good about Growing Up Pan £2.99
A witty but wise guide to the physical, emotional and sexual changes which are part of growing up. 'A gold mine of good advice and plain facts which makes growing up seem so much easier.' (Dr Alan Maryon Davis)

Sharpe, Sue
Falling for Love: Teenage Mothers Talk. Virago £3.99.
Young mothers tell their own stories of boyfriends, parents, schoolfriends and teachers.

Shaw, Dr Phyllis
Meeting People is Fun: How to Overcome Shyness. Sheldon Press £3.99.
Recognizing the problems and learning to deal with them by self-help and support from others.

Thomson, Ruth
Have You Started Yet? Pan £3.50.
Menstruation and how to cope with it.

Carol Weston
Girltalk Pan £4.99
Revised
This down-to-earth book for girls gives advice on family, friendships, school, sex, drink, drugs, health, money and making the most of life.